RENTAL CAR DECISIONS

WHAT YOU DON'T KNOW CAN HURT YOU

DENNIS STUTH

Auto Risk Resources Press
Bourbonnais, IL

Published by Auto Risk Resources Press
P.O. Box 904
Bourbonnais, IL 60914

Publisher's Cataloguing-in-Publication Data
Stuth, Dennis.

Rental car decisions : what you don't know can hurt you / Dennis Stuth. – Bourbonnais, IL : Auto Risk Resources Press, 2005.

p. ; cm.
ISBN: 0-9753338-0-1

1. Rental automobiles. 2. Automobile leasing and renting–United States–Corrupt practices. 3. Lease and rental services–United States–Corrupt practices. 4. Consumer protection. I. Title.

HD9710.25 .S882 2005   2004109468
388.3/42/0973–dc22   CIP

Book production coordination by Jenkins Group, Inc. www.bookpublishing.com
Interior Design by Chad Miller/Fourteen Little Men
Cover Design by Chris Rhoads
Printed in United States of America
09 08 07 06 05 • 5 4 3 2 1

WARNING AND DISCLAIMER

This book is designed to provide information in regard to the subject matter covered. It is sold with the understanding that the author and publisher are not engaged in rendering legal, financial or other professional services. If legal or other such assistance is required, the services of a competent professional should be sought.

Every effort has been made to make this book as complete and as accurate as possible. However, there may be mistakes both typographical and in content. Therefore, this text should be used only as a general guide and not as the ultimate source on the subject. Furthermore, this book contains information on the subject only up to the printing date.

The purpose of this text is to inform and educate. The author and Auto Risk Resources Press shall have neither liability nor responsibility to any person or entity with respect to any loss or damage caused or alleged to be caused directly or indirectly by the information contained in this book. When in doubt, consult with your attorney.

Laws and regulations relative to the subject matter may change. The author cannot predict what legislatures and courts may decide after this book is printed.

If you do not agree with the above, you may return this book to the publisher for a full refund.

DEDICATION

To Teresa, for her love and inspiration in helping make this project a reality.

To Taryn, Brandon and Tanner, for adding so much joy and happiness to my life.

To my parents, for a lifetime of encouragement and support.

CONTENTS

Introduction

Remember the first time you rented a car? You probably walked away from the rental counter with your head spinning and a queasy feeling in the pit of your stomach. You may have already been a little apprehensive about traveling, only to find that what you expected to be a relatively simple transaction ended up making you feel rather uncomfortable and uninformed.

Moments earlier, you found yourself face-to-face with a rental agent who was firing questions at you that you had no idea how to answer. You were in a hurry and didn't have time to ask many questions or seek clarification. Even if you had, you would have felt self-conscious doing so with a long line of people behind you. Before you realized what was happening, you were asked to provide your driver's license and credit card, initial here, and sign there, and you were on your way with the keys to your rental car in hand.

When you were finally able to reflect on what had taken place, you may have felt a little annoyed that the rental agent seemed to force you to dig deeper into your pocket by suggesting vehicle upgrades, optional insurance, and other features. You wondered why none of this was explained or even mentioned when you made your reservation.

Perhaps you even felt somewhat angry that the intent of the agent seemed to have been more focused on generating a larger sale than on providing the level of information and service you needed. You came away with the perception that it had been the rental company's plan to "put one over on you."

I also experienced these very feelings the first time I rented a car and wondered why a seemingly simple process had to be made so difficult and confusing. Not until I went to work for a car rental company was I able to get some answers.

As an industry insider, I learned about the huge financial risks that car rental companies take on in exchange for a small profit margin. When you think about it, it does seem to be a pretty foolish business. After all, would you hand over the keys to your personal auto that might be worth $20,000, $30,000, or more to a stranger in exchange for $30 or $40 per day, not knowing for sure how your vehicle would be driven or even whether you'd ever see it again?

Car rental companies do just that millions of times each year, and they rely only upon a couple of forms of identification provided by customers. The cost is an incredible bargain when you consider that you might pay $100 a day to rent a tuxedo worth $500 but can rent a $30,000 car for less than $50 a day. Think about it—the cost of renting a car is often less than renting a handheld power tool!

But even if you fully understand that the huge financial risk faced by the rental companies necessitates the complexity of the transaction, one question still remains: why haven't rental companies done a better job of educating customers to help them understand the rental process?

Several years ago, a commentary titled "A Proposal for Cleaning up the Industry's Image" appeared in an issue of *Auto Rental News*, an industry publication. It described the rental industry's image problem and listed some suggestions for improvement. More than anything else, this commentary underscored the need for customer education.

In measuring its overall performance in terms of customer satisfaction, the car rental industry has too often focused on factors such as the frequency of shuttle busses and the speed of the pickup and return processes. As a result, the industry has worked long and hard on improving those parts of the process.

But although speed and convenience factors are important to most customers, perhaps the "image problem" discussed in the article is more closely related to the industry's failure to effectively educate customers about the actual process of renting a car.

The article identified some negative perceptions shared by many customers, including:

- Insurance options are too numerous, expensive, and confusing.
- There is too much industry terminology used in describing these options.
- The extent of your responsibility for vehicle damage and liability is confusing.
- There are too many "hidden" charges that make it hard to know how much you'll actually be paying for the rental.
- The rental contract is difficult to read and understand.
- Customers are not instructed in the operation of the vehicle's equipment.

- The business processes and practices of the industry are generally difficult for customers to understand.

What has the industry done to overcome these criticisms? Following this article, the American Car Rental Association (ACRA) published a list of 10 car rental tips designed to assist customers. The list included such suggestions as:

- Understand optional waivers
- Review optional insurance products
- Review fueling options

Not exactly priceless advice, is it? It is probably safe to assume that most car rental customers already identified these as issues. What they want is someone to *help them better understand these issues!*

This failure to make the rental process simpler for customers sometimes leads to the belief that the industry "has something to hide." Articles have been written about how the industry tries to confuse customers and "gouge" them with overpriced add-ons, options, and hidden charges. Governmental regulators have even started keeping a closer watch on certain industry practices, such as insurance sales.

Will the rental companies ever act to reverse this perception? The *Auto Rental News* commentary makes a number of suggestions for doing so, such as trying to simplify some of these more confusing issues and providing customers with sufficient information to make educated decisions. But will the industry ever follow this advice?

The industry does not intentionally try to mislead the public or keep its customers uninformed. It simply fails to recognize the benefit of educating its customers. It remains focused on factors such as rates and convenience. It continues to believe that all customers treat car rental as a commodity, with purchase decisions based solely on price.

But maybe there also exists a fear that educated consumers might become less likely to accept some of the add-ons the companies now offer if the customers had a better understanding of the process. Could the industry be afraid that educated customers might make better buying decisions, thus cutting further into the already thin profit margins?

Regardless of the industry's motivation (or lack thereof), it is probably unrealistic to expect rental companies to put any of the proposed solutions to this problem in place. Consider the following reasons why any significant action is unlikely:

- Issues such as optional insurance protection and rental contract language are, by their very nature, very complex. Getting customers to clearly understand these matters is no easy task.
- There is an inherent conflict between the desire to adequately inform customers and the goal of decreasing the time they spend at the rental counter. No one wants customers to stand in line for long periods while the rental agent goes through lengthy explanations.
- The industry has not found an effective way to communicate information to customers before they reach the rental counter. Considering that a sizable percentage of customers fails to show up and honor reservations, each second of time spent on the phone at the reservation stage becomes costly.
- Providing additional printed material to customers is impractical. Companies rely upon their rental contract language to define their duties and responsibilities, as well as those of the renter. Providing additional written information might create conflicts with contract language or ambiguities and might diminish the enforceability of the contract's provisions.
- Even if companies wanted to provide customers with specific information outlining their responsibilities and available options, the process would be expensive and difficult to administer because of state laws that govern the rental transaction. Companies would need to produce many different versions and make sure that the right version was given to each customer.
- The car rental companies make quite a bit of money by selling products such as optional protection. Some are more aggressive than others in their sales efforts, but they all earn significant income from these sales. Some of these sales come from customers who really might not need the extra protection. Educating the customer could cause current revenue levels to fall.

The track record of the rental industry shows that it has not been very eager to explain its business practices to customers, the media, consumer groups, or regulators. There is little reason to think that this trend will change much in the near future.

But if the rental companies aren't going to help you, how are you supposed to obtain the information you need to gain a better understanding of the car rental process? From the media perhaps? Numerous newspaper and magazine articles providing advice on renting a car have been written by travel and consumer information writers. Although these writers are very well informed on many travel topics, most do not possess the specialized knowledge required to address some of the more complex issues related to renting a car.

In fact, there are many examples of such car rental advice actually being incorrect. In some cases, the misinformation has been relatively harmless. In others, the advice could have become quite costly to a customer who followed it.

This is not a criticism of the authors of these articles. By necessity, most need to be travel generalists who dispense helpful tips about a myriad of general travel topics. But regardless of one's travel experience, even the best of the travel writers cannot possess the same level of expertise about car rental issues as does an industry insider.

The problem is by no means limited to travel writers. Insurance agents dread getting questions from their policyholders about car rental insurance issues. Travel agents aren't sure what to tell customers who ask whether they need to buy extra rental insurance. Corporate travel and risk managers struggle with the task of developing integrated insurance programs that effectively protect against the car rental exposure. Insurance claims adjusters don't fully understand what coverage is provided under the terms of the rental contract and how it interacts with their policies.

So where is a rental customer or professional responsible for giving rental advice to turn? The obvious answer is to someone who has worked in the industry—an insider with years of practical experience and knowledge, one with knowledge not only of rental operations but also more importantly of insurance-related matters because that's where much of the confusion exists.

This book will not offer tips on how to find the best rate or which company to use. Instead, it will provide practical information to give you a better overall understanding of the rental process. It will inform you of your responsibilities and the potential financial risks faced when renting a car. It will explain which optional coverages you as a renter may or may not need. It will also help lead you through the rental contract maze by clarifying what its provisions really mean. It will teach you how to better ensure your safety as a renter as well as the safety of your passengers.

Simply stated, this book has two objectives. The first is to show renters how to better protect themselves financially. The second is to help those professionals who deal with rental issues become more knowledgeable and effective in their jobs.

chapter one

Does It Have to Be So Complicated?

Let's first look at some reasons why the process of renting a car has to be so complicated. In many respects, car rental is much more complex than most other forms of transportation. When you travel by bus, train, airplane, taxi, or cruise ship, you simply make your reservation, pay your fare, and show up on time. There's not much more to worry about.

Renting a car puts you in a completely different and unfamiliar situation. You have far more freedom and flexibility than with any other mode of transportation because it is the only time you are actually given total control of the equipment used to transport you. But as soon as you assume physical possession of your rental car, you immediately take on certain significant duties and responsibilities relating to the use of that vehicle.

Those duties and responsibilities arise out of exactly what makes renting a car unique— the transfer of control of the vehicle from the rental company to the customer. Once the rental company relinquishes physical control to you, it also transfers some of the financial exposures associated with its operation. If you don't recognize and understand those financial exposures, it can cost you.

How do you determine what your duties and responsibilities are? Ask a car rental reservation or counter agent and you'll be told that they are "clearly" described on the rental contract. To make matters worse, you'll also be required to sign the rental contract before they give you the keys, and you need to acknowledge that you have read and understand these duties.

Have you ever tried to read the small print on a rental contract? Even if you were able to comprehend all of the language and terminology, would you ever take the time required to read the entire agreement while standing at the rental counter with a schedule to keep and a long line of impatient customers behind you?

Faced with this impossible task, most car rental customers show full and complete trust in the rental company by simply signing their names and initialing in the spaces where they are told on the contract in order to get their car and be their way.

Few customers realize that signing that agreement exposes them to an area in which they probably have little familiarity: contractual liability. If they have an accident, they'll quickly learn that their financial responsibility for that accident will be determined not only by the degree to which they were at fault but also by the liability they agreed to assume when they signed the rental contract.

This contractual liability can include responsibility for damage to the rental vehicle as well as for the bodily injury and property damage claims made by other parties involved in the accident (often referred to as "third parties"). Many first-time renters fail to understand that they will be held responsible for all damage to the rental vehicle, even if the accident was not their fault.

Neither are many renters aware that they may have significant exposure for liability claims by third parties. Most U.S. residents are aware of the usual "insurance follows the car" rule prevalent in this country. However, with rental cars, applicable laws sometimes require that the insurance instead "follows the driver."

Confused yet? Maybe even a little frightened about getting behind the wheel of a rental car again? If so, don't worry. That's a good sign. Of the millions of people who rent cars each year, most are not confused or frightened simply because they don't understand the potential financial risks they face. Just remember that the difference between a pleasant rental experience and one that ends in disaster can be dependent on (1) your level of knowledge about the financial risks you face when renting a car and (2) what you do to make certain that you are adequately protected.

7

Some travel articles have described "unpleasant rental experiences" in which renters discover that they paid a higher rate than needed, didn't get the vehicle they reserved, or had to wait long periods at the rental counter. These problems represent mere inconveniences when compared with discovering that you are financially responsible for damage to a $30,000 vehicle or being faced with a multimillion-dollar liability lawsuit. Those are truly unpleasant rental experiences!

Yet issues relating to a renter's potential financial exposure are rarely addressed. No one writes articles about people facing huge court judgments because they didn't have adequate liability coverage when they rented a car.

This, in part, answers the question of why the rental process has to be so complex. When the rental company hands over the keys to one of its vehicles to a customer, the transaction exposes both parties to significant financial risks that need to be clarified. To carefully spell out the duties and responsibilities of each party requires a very detailed, precise, and unambiguous contract.

One of the primary purposes of the rental contract is to limit the potential financial exposure of the rental company by transferring some of that exposure to the customer. But the contract also serves to limit the renter's responsibilities by clearly defining them. In the absence of a written contract, renters could be surprised to learn after the fact about additional responsibilities (and possibly charges) that were not identified at the time of rental. The rental contract serves as the foundation for the rental transaction between the company and the customer.

But does the rental contract have to be so complicated and confusing? Even if the complexity of the rental transaction requires the use of "small print legalese," why can't the rental companies at least make it easier to understand?

Companies may be reluctant to produce customer-friendly material that uses plain language to explain their contracts for fear of creating potential ambiguities that could work to their detriment. As in the case of most contracts, ambiguities are generally resolved in favor of the party that did not participate in the writing of the contract. In that respect, the rental contract is considered a "contract of adhesion" because it is drafted by the rental company and offered to the customer on essentially a "take it or leave it" basis. The customer has no ability to negotiate the terms of the contract and usually cannot rent a vehicle without acquiescing to the contract as written. Therefore, any ambiguity would likely be decided in favor of the customer.

In the material that follows, we will attempt to demystify the rental contract and provide you with a greater understanding of some of the common and more important provisions. However, in reviewing this material, it is necessary to understand that our explanation of rental contract terms must be somewhat general in nature.

Although we would like to be able to address every specific policy, procedure, and variation of rental contract language that exists in the industry, it is impossible to do for several reasons:

- Rental contract terms and conditions vary from one company to another.
- Rental contract terms and conditions can vary even within the same company depending on rental location.
- Rental companies often change the language of their rental contracts without public notice.
- Some states have enacted specific car rental statutes whose provisions will prevail over any conflicting rental contract terms.

The objective will be to provide you with enough insights and recommendations that will allow you to know where to look for key information and make informed decisions regardless of any variations in contract language.

Before beginning a discussion of rental contract terms and conditions, it is necessary to first gain a general understanding some of the more significant financial exposures faced by both the rental company and the customer. Describing the loss exposures faced by the rental companies first will enable you to better understand why and how they try to shift many of their exposures to you, the customer.

LOSS EXPOSURES FACED BY CAR RENTAL COMPANIES

In order to fully appreciate the purpose of the rental contract, it is necessary to have a general understanding of what the rental company is trying to accomplish. Its principal objective is to minimize the potential loss exposures it faces when renting cars to the public. Being aware of what those exposures are will help explain the rationale behind much of the contract.

First, let's define what we mean by "loss exposure." For our purposes, a "loss exposure" will be defined as the potential for financial loss to the rental company that can arise out of an accident or incident associated with its business of renting cars. The main loss exposures faced by rental companies include:

Loss of or damage to the rental vehicle

One of the largest financial exposures to a rental company is that associated with the loss of or damage to its rental vehicles. This loss can range from minor damage such as body scratches and cracked windshields to the theft or total loss of the vehicle.

In some cases, the cost of vehicle damage losses sustained by the rental company can be recovered from either a third party who is legally liable for the accident or from the renter who assumed that responsibility under the terms of the rental contract. Whenever possible, the rental company will pursue all possible means of recovery to minimize its vehicle damage losses.

But sometimes the cost of vehicle damage cannot be recovered. The party responsible for the accident may not have insurance or other assets. Sometimes, the rental company discovers damage and cannot determine when it occurred or who is responsible. When recovery is not possible, the rental company must either rely upon its own fleet insurance or, if it has no fleet insurance, absorb the damage amount as a cost of doing business.

Loss of revenue while the rental vehicle is out of service (loss of use)

This loss exposure is closely associated with vehicle damage. Whenever a rental vehicle is out of service for repairs, the rental company obviously cannot rent it. The vehicle becomes an asset that is no longer capable of producing revenue until its repairs are complete and it is returned to service.

The rental company will attempt to recover any lost revenue from those responsible for causing the damage to the rental vehicle. But as in the case of the vehicle damage exposure, that cost is not always recoverable.

Administrative costs related to the handling of accident claims

When a rental car is involved in an accident, there are some costs associated with the administration and handling of the claim. Someone needs to complete an accident report, enter the accident into a claim database, set up a claim file, investigate the facts of the accident, estimate the vehicle damage, and perform other related tasks.

These functions are not directly related to the business of renting cars but must still be performed when accidents occur, with the cost borne by the rental company. These administrative costs would not occur if not for an accident.

Depending on applicable state law, rental companies sometimes attempt recovery of the administrative costs associated with vehicle damage claims.

Some states have specific laws or regulations defining the extent to which administrative costs may be recovered.

Costs incurred by rental companies for the handling of liability claims are generally not recoverable and are considered a cost of doing business.

Legal liability to third parties arising from ownership of rental vehicles
As owners of the vehicles, rental companies are obligated by law to fulfill certain financial responsibility or compulsory liability requirements. These laws are intended to ensure that the victims of accidents are adequately compensated by those legally liable for their damages. Each state establishes a minimum limit of liability (or financial responsibility requirement) that must be met either by means of an insurance policy or through a qualified self-insurance program.

In the past, these state financial responsibility laws imposed the primary liability responsibility on the owner of the vehicle (the rental company). However, rental companies have been relatively successful in shifting that responsibility to the renter (or other authorized operator) by means of the language used in rental contracts. Either by authority of statute or applicable case law, most states now allow this shifting of primary liability responsibility to the renter or other authorized operator of the rental vehicle.

The rental industry initiated this contractual transfer or shifting of financial responsibility to the renter in the early 1990s in an effort to control skyrocketing liability costs. The rationale was that had the industry not done this, liability costs would have ultimately been passed on in the form of higher rates to all customers, not just to those who had accidents.

Although quite controversial at the time, the industry felt this shifting to be in the best interest of the majority of customers for several reasons:
- Because most rental customers are never involved in an accident, receiving a lower rental rate is clearly beneficial to the vast majority of renters.
- Customers are already paying for liability protection that will cover them in a rental car under their personal or business insurance policies. If the rental company passed accident costs on in the form of higher rental rates, customers would actually be paying for the same protection twice.

- Customers having a direct financial interest probably tend to operate the rental vehicle with a higher degree of care than if totally free of responsibility. This self-imposed "loss control" helps contain costs for both the renter and rental company, not to mention that it helps keep the roads a little safer.

Legal liability to third parties arising from maintenance of rental vehicles

Rental companies are also responsible for providing customers with vehicles that are mechanically safe. If an accident occurs and it is shown that the vehicle malfunctioned because of a defect that the company failed to identify or because the vehicle had been improperly maintained, the company may be held directly liable for any damages.

Allegations of improper maintenance or mechanical failure, whether warranted, are often raised in claims involving serious injuries. This occurs when a plaintiff attorney, realizing that a client's recovery will be limited to the applicable state financial responsibility limit (which is typically quite low) provided under the terms of the rental contract, seeks a "deep pocket" to pursue. The potential recovery in a direct cause of action claim against the rental company on the basis of this type of allegation is unlimited, so the plaintiff suddenly has a much bigger target.

The rental companies are often able to defeat these allegations but not without considerable effort and expense. So whether a claim of improper maintenance is successful, the financial cost to a rental company remains significant, at least in terms of the cost to defend.

Legal liability to third parties arising from the process of renting vehicles

The rental process represents another potential loss exposure. Rental companies are responsible for exercising proper care in entrusting vehicles to their customers. If a rental company rents a car to an individual who does not possess a valid driver's license or who comes to pick up a car in an obviously intoxicated state, the company could be held responsible if that individual causes an accident while operating the rental car.

For this reason, rental companies maintain certain requirements and qualifications for their prospective customers. Failing to establish such criteria or failing to enforce those criteria could expose the rental company to potentially large judgments.

LOSS EXPOSURES FACED BY THE CAR RENTAL CUSTOMER

The preceding discussion of rental company exposures lays a foundation on which it becomes easier to understand the exposures faced by you as a rental customer. In many respects, you face many of the same exposures when renting a vehicle that you face while operating your personal vehicle. The big difference comes from the fact that when renting a car, you also assume some additional exposures under the terms of the rental contract. The exposures assumed under the rental contract are the result of the rental company trying to transfer some of its exposures to you.

The principal loss exposures you face when renting a car include:

Financial responsibility for loss of or damage to the rental vehicle

The terms of the rental contract hold you personally responsible for any and all damage that occurs to the rental vehicle during the rental period. You are required to return the rental vehicle in the same condition as when you took possession, except for ordinary wear and tear.

Rental companies are usually not too forgiving in terms of their definition of "wear and tear." You may feel that minor dents, scratches, and dings should fall within that definition. The rental company may not agree, and you may find yourself being billed for what you consider to be minor damage.

Your responsibility for vehicle damage is not limited to the damage to the vehicle caused by your negligence. You will also be held responsible for all damage even when another party was at fault and you are completely free of negligence. Any damage ultimately becomes your responsibility regardless of how it occurred.

Diminution in value

Rental companies sometimes attempt to pursue claims for the "diminished value" of a vehicle that results from its being damaged in an accident. They claim that if the vehicle's resale value is adversely affected because of damage (even if it has been repaired correctly), the company may look to the customer for the difference in resale value as part of its vehicle damage claim.

This issue is currently the subject of litigation throughout the country. At this time, some states have case law holding that a claim for diminution in value is valid. Courts in other states have decided that such claims are without merit. In still yet others, there exists no relevant case law, and the issue has not yet been decided.

Financial responsibility for loss of use and administrative costs

The terms of the rental contract also hold you responsible for revenue lost by the rental company resulting from its inability to rent the damaged vehicle while it is undergoing repairs or while it is out of service. You may also be held responsible for certain administrative costs incurred by the rental company in arranging repairs, handling the vehicle damage claim, and pursuing recovery of the damage amount.

Legal liability for third-party bodily injury and property damage claims that result from your use or operation of the rental vehicle

Your legal liability for damages to others resulting from your operation of the rental car is, in essence, similar to your exposure while operating your own personal vehicle.

The legal liability of the operator of a motor vehicle is based on the concept of negligence. Negligence is founded in tort law and can be defined as a private, or civil, wrong (as distinguished from a public, or criminal, wrong) against another party for which the law provides remedies. It is the basis for auto liability claims and allows for the recovery of monetary damages as remedy.

To prove negligence against a vehicle operator, it is necessary to show a duty (to drive in a safe, responsible manner and in compliance with all motor vehicle laws), a breach of that duty (the operator's the failure to do so), and the resulting damages that another party suffered as a direct and proximate result of that breach.

Damages may include medical expenses, loss of earnings, pain and suffering, and property damage. As stated above, the remedy is a monetary award intended to adequately compensate the damaged party.

If you are found to be legally liable for an accident resulting from your use or operation of the rental car, you will have financial responsibility for any resultant injuries or damages. The issue then becomes identifying potential sources of liability coverage that are available to you (i.e., personal or business auto liability insurance) and whether that coverage becomes primary or secondary to the protection provided by the rental company under the terms of the rental contract.

Medical expenses for injuries to you or your passengers while occupying the rental vehicle

If you are injured while operating or occupying your rental vehicle, you could have responsibility for any resultant medical expenses. Depending on your degree of legal liability for an accident, you could also bear some potential responsibility for any medical expenses of passengers in your rental car.

Loss of or damage to personal property contained in the rental vehicle

Personal property owned by you or your passengers could be damaged or stolen while located in your rental car. This could result in a financial loss unless the property is fully covered by insurance. In most cases, you will at least be responsible for a deductible even if the property is insured.

By now, you are hopefully starting to understand some of the reasons for the complexity of the rental transaction. The potential financial exposures faced by both the rental companies and the rental customers are significant. To clarify each party's duties and responsibilities as they relate to these exposures, a very clear and concise contract becomes necessary.

Your financial exposures as a rental customer will be described in more detail in Chapters 5 and 6. But before venturing into the world of car rental financial exposures and insurance issues, it is necessary to explain some important aspects of the rental process.

chapter two

Will They Rent to You?

The previous chapter explained how the business of renting cars represents a significant financial risk to a car rental company. It hands over the keys to an expensive vehicle and knows only a few bits of information about the customer. It doesn't know whether the customer will operate the car in a responsible manner or abuse it. It doesn't know whether the vehicle will be returned in the same condition or even whether it will ever be seen again. If it is returned with damage, it doesn't know whether the customer will be able to pay for the damage.

For these reasons, rental companies try to be a little careful about who they accept as customers. Most have established criteria designed to help them identify the customers most likely to have accidents or damage their vehicles. The companies refer to this as the "qualification" process in which they match certain customer characteristics against industry standards to determine whether the customer qualifies for rental.

The criteria most frequently used by rental companies to qualify customers include:

- Age
- Possession of a valid driver's license
- Driving record
- Method of payment

AGE

Most rental companies impose a minimum age requirement, meaning that customers younger than the stated minimum age are not allowed to rent.

This restriction is intended to help reduce the rental company's accident rate. Statistics clearly show that youthful drivers have a much higher incidence of motor vehicle crashes than does any other age segment. They also indicate that not only do young drivers have more accidents, but also their accidents are more serious. A National Highway Traffic Safety Administration (NHTSA) study for the year 2001 showed that drivers under 25 years of age had the highest rate of involvement in fatal auto crashes of any age group.

There are a number of reasons for the high accident rate for young drivers. Studies have shown excessive speed to be a leading factor in many accidents involving young drivers. This probably results from the general sense of invincibility and tendency toward risk taking and "showing off" that seems common at that age. The use of alcohol has also been found to be a factor in many serious accidents involving young drivers. Finally, there exists a relatively low incidence of safety belt use among young drivers.

As a result, many car rental companies have set their minimum age requirement at 25. Some companies will rent to customers under 25 but may then impose other restrictions or surcharges.

For example, a company might generally rent to customers under 25, but it might refuse to do so at certain times of the year such as during spring break or prom season. Rental companies may also restrict the type of vehicle that a young customer can rent. It may be acceptable to rent a four-cylinder economy car but not a convertible sports car.

When a young driver surcharge is imposed, that fee can be quite high. A driver under 25 years of age can expect to pay from $10 to $50 or more over the daily rental charge for the privilege of renting a vehicle. The actual amount of the young driver surcharge will depend on the rental location, the type of vehicle, and the age of the renter.

During the early 1990s, many rental companies raised their minimum age requirement from 21 to 25 in response to rising accident costs. This change was challenged as discriminatory in some courts, most notably in the state of New York.

In 1997, the New York Court of Appeals ruled that car rental companies could not refuse to rent to anyone 18 years of age or older solely based upon their age unless the companies could prove that insurance for this age segment was unavailable. If insurance was available, companies were authorized to add the cost of such insurance to the rental transaction.

The result has been that most companies operating in New York do rent to customers from age 18 to 24, but they also add on a rather hefty surcharge. Although some may argue that age restrictions and surcharges are discriminatory, it is difficult to dispute that this age group does have significantly higher accident costs than does the average renter.

Interestingly, rental companies do not apply a maximum age restriction in the United States despite statistics that show accident costs for drivers over 70 also to be high. Apparently, car rental companies recognize the political implications of turning away senior citizens and have stayed away from that potential controversy.

There is one notable exception to the minimum age requirement restriction used by most car rental companies. If a rental company has a corporate agreement with a business customer, the customer's employees typically do not have to satisfy the 25 years of age requirement.

Imposing an age restriction on business customers would become problematic if young employees who needed to travel to perform their jobs were unable to rent a car. In addition to obvious business implications, car rental companies also reason that young drivers who are renting within the scope of their employment are less likely to operate the vehicle in an irresponsible manner.

POSSESSION OF A VALID DRIVER'S LICENSE

It seems obvious that car rental companies would require all renters to have a valid driver's license. Operating a motor vehicle without a license is in violation of state law, and rental companies do not want to put someone behind the wheel who may not be competent. Although a driver's license may not be a guarantee that an individual is a safe driver, it at least serves as verification that the person passed some type of test and received state approval to drive.

There is another important reason for requiring a valid driver's license. The license serves as a valuable piece of identification and information. At the very least, the license helps the rental agent verify the identity of the customer.

You are usually required to present your driver's license at the time of rental. The rental agent will examine the license and will pay particular attention to:

- Your name (to verify that it is consistent with the information on your reservation and credit card)
- Your photo (to help confirm your identify)
- Your physical description (your height, weight, and hair and eye color)
- Your date of birth (to determine whether you meet the minimum age requirement)
- Your signature (to make sure it matches the signature on your other forms of identification as well as on the rental contract)

The agent will also check the expiration date on the license. Your license must not only be valid at the time of rental but also must remain valid throughout the entire rental period. If it will expire during the rental period, you will not be allowed to rent.

The rental agent will also look for any sign that the license may have been altered. If any evidence that the license has been modified exists, you may be turned away.

The driver's license requirement is not always simple and clear cut. There are many variables as well as some differences in the way that rental companies treat this issue.

In looking at this requirement in greater detail, driver's licenses issued in the United States and those issued by other countries will be addressed separately.

Driver's licenses issued in the United States

This category includes licenses issued by any of the 50 states as well as in U.S. territories and possessions. In addition to a permanent, state-issued driver's license, the following types of licenses may be acceptable:

- **Temporary license:** Some states issue temporary licenses that can be used until the permanent license is issued. A temporary license is usually acceptable provided that it will remain valid throughout the entire rental period.
- **Traffic citation or ticket:** Some states allow drivers to surrender their licenses in lieu of posting a bond when cited for minor traffic violations. The paper citation, or traffic ticket, is often considered to be a valid license until the disposition of the citation and the return of

the permanent license. When the issuing state recognizes a citation as a valid license, rental companies will usually accept the citation unless it is for a serious violation such as DUI or reckless driving. When a citation or ticket is accepted, the rental company may also require an additional form of photo identification.

- **U.S. Military ID card:** Individuals serving in the military sometimes allow their driver's licenses to expire while on active duty. For those individuals, rental companies may accept the expired license along with proof of active duty.

A few other general rules in regards to the driver's license requirement:

- A learner's permit is not considered a valid license.
- Excuses for not producing a valid license will not be accepted. If you forgot your license at home or lost it that morning, you will be out of luck.
- Rental companies typically do not pay attention to license restrictions. For example, if your license restricts your driving to daylight hours, the rental company will assume that you will abide by that restriction.

Driver's licenses issued by other countries

Customers residing outside of the United States are required to present a valid license issued by their home country that is valid during the entire rental period.

For licenses issued outside of the United States, the following rules generally apply:

- Licenses issued by the renter's home country usually satisfy the license requirement without additional documentation when the license is in English.
- When the license is written in a language other than English, some rental companies also require an international driver's permit (IDP).
- An IDP alone is generally not acceptable. It must be accompanied by the actual driver's license issued by the renter's home country.
- When the driver's license does not include a photo, the renter may be asked to also produce another form of photo ID.
- Licenses from most foreign countries are accepted, but some rental companies restrict their list to countries that are signatories of the United Nations Convention on Road Traffic or the Convention on the Regulation of InterAmerican Automotive Traffic. (Most countries participate in one or both of these agreements.)

- Some companies may require a passport in addition to a driver's license from the customer's home country.

DRIVING RECORD

A renter is also required to have an "acceptable" driving record. This requirement was also implemented during the early 1990s in response to escalating accident costs. As companies searched to find ways to contain these costs, the concept of applying some basic insurance "underwriting" standards to rental customers was adopted.

One of the most basic underwriting principles is that an individual's past driving history is a strong predictor of future accident activity. Prior to the early 1990s, the strong industry emphasis on market share and revenue precluded most types of customer screening. Rapidly increasing accident costs then caused rental companies to rethink that strategy and begin trying to identify customer segments with higher-risk profiles.

How do the rental companies obtain information about your driving record? Basically, this is accomplished in one of two ways:

Driving record questionnaire
The rental company may ask you to fill out a brief form that contains questions about your driving history. The form will ask about your driving violation convictions and at-fault accidents. On the basis of your answers, the rental agent will determine whether you meet the company's standards and qualify for rental.

Although it would seem easy for a renter to simply lie about his or her driving record, the potential repercussions would be severe. These questionnaire forms are considered to be part of the rental contract, so any misrepresentation or false information may be considered a violation of the contract's terms and could void any protection that would otherwise be available. So though lying about your driving record might enable you to drive off in a rental car, it could become quite costly to you in the event of an accident.

How does a renter who lies get caught? Some companies will randomly spot-check customers who have completed the form by obtaining their official driving record from the state. Other companies will check the records of all renters who completed a form and later had an accident. If the individual's state record reveals that he or she provided false information in filling out the form, the company will consider it to be a violation of the rental contract.

Refusing to complete a driving record questionnaire when requested to do so will result in not being allowed to rent a car.

Automated driving record checks

The second way rental companies review your driving history is by means of an automated online check of your record. This is accomplished through a very sophisticated process in which the rental agent submits your driver's license number to a vendor that is connected to the Department of Motor Vehicles (DMV) of various states. The vendor obtains your driving record (called a motor vehicle record, or MVR) from your state's DMV and then matches your record with the driving record criteria set by the rental company. On the basis of the information on your record and the company's criteria, the vendor sends either a "rent" or a "do not rent" message back to the rental company.

This entire process typically takes less than five seconds and is usually transparent to the rental customer. Most customers are unaware that the process is even taking place unless they are among the unfortunate few who "fail" the screening. On average, between 5% and 10% of customers whose records are electronically checked do not pass.

When this screening process was first introduced (also during the early 1990s), it was met with much negative media and public reaction. One complaint was that it was in violation of that customer's privacy, but the state record used in the screening process is public information. Furthermore, the rental agent does not actually see the customer's driving record or any other personal information about the customer beyond that listed on the driver's license. The only information that the agent receives is a "rent" or a "do not rent" message from the vendor.

Some failing customers complained that because the driving record check was performed at the time of rental, they were left stranded at the rental location. They felt that the screening should instead be done at the time of reservation so they would know in advance whether they would be turned down for rental. From a cost perspective, this was not practical because the fees charged by the states for these records are relatively expensive, and a significant number of customers fail to show up for their reservation.

As time has passed, negative public reaction has diminished, possibly in recognition of the need to keep unsafe drivers off the road and to maintain the lowest possible rental rates for the majority of customers who are good drivers.

Most rental companies do not perform the automated screening process at all rental locations. They will sometimes decide to use it only in areas where they are experiencing above-average accident frequency.

Other factors that enter into the decision of when to use automated driver screening are the volume of customers the location has from states providing online access and the MVR fees charged by those states. In many cases, it becomes a business decision based on a cost/benefit analysis. It is also not uncommon for rental companies to change the list of locations using the process from time to time.

DRIVING RECORDS CRITERIA

Rental companies utilizing automated driving record screening each develop their own set of criteria based on business needs. Although the criteria may vary to some degree by company, the following are those most commonly used to disqualify potential renters:

- **Driver's license currently expired, suspended, revoked, invalid, or surrendered**

  Surprisingly, this is often a leading reason that customers fail. Some studies have found that roughly 2% of all customers checked did not have a valid driver's license despite the fact that they were required to display one at the rental counter. This situation can occur in states that don't physically confiscate licenses that have been suspended or revoked. As a result, an individual can continue to use a driver's license as identification even though the state no longer recognizes its validity. In addition, some licenses that are presented are found to be fraudulent or counterfeit.

- **Conviction for driving under the influence of alcohol or other controlled substance**

  These offenses include driving while intoxicated (DWI), driving under the influence of alcohol or other controlled substance (DUI), and driving while alcohol impaired (DWAI). One conviction within the previous 36 months will often disqualify a customer, although some companies use periods up to 72 months.

- **Conviction for other major violations**

  Other major violations may include such offenses as reckless driving, failure to report an accident, leaving the scene of an accident, fleeing or eluding a police officer, and use of a vehicle in a crime. Again, one

23

conviction within a specified period (usually ranging between 36 and 72 months) will cause an individual to fail.

- **Convictions for a specified number of minor violations**
  These violations may include such offenses as failure to obey a traffic control, failure to yield the right of way, improper turn, improper lane use, and speeding. (Some companies consider speeding to be a major violation when it is significantly above the limit.) In recognition of the fact that many drivers do get an occasional traffic ticket, this criterion is somewhat more forgiving, with three or more convictions during a specified period usually required to disqualify a customer.
- **Involvement in a specified number or type of accidents within a certain period**
  This generally applies only to individuals having driver's licenses from states that list accidents on their MVRs. Not all state driving records show accidents, and those that do include accident information may not give any indication of fault.
- **Conviction for possession of a stolen vehicle**
  The fact that rental car companies wish to avoid doing business with anyone convicted of this offense probably requires no further explanation.

Some customers who fail will claim that the information contained in their state driving record is incorrect. Be aware that the rental company will consider that information to be official and will usually not change its rental decision. If the state record does actually contain an error, it is the customer's responsibility to contact the DMV to get it corrected.

There are some limitations to qualifying customers on the basis of their driving records. It can be done only for customers with driver's licenses issued in the United States because the rental companies have no means of checking driving records from outside of the country. Also, certain customers may be exempted from the process, such as employees of companies that have corporate agreements with the rental company.

METHOD OF PAYMENT

Assuming that the rental company has done an effective job in weeding out those customers most likely to have an accident, it still is not done in the qualification process. The last step is to make certain that the customer will be able to pay the rental charges.

Customers may be allowed to pay for their rental in any of several ways including:

- Credit cards
- Debit cards
- Vouchers
- Direct billing
- Cash

This can sometimes get confusing because although rental companies may accept each of these as payment options, they may not accept them in qualifying for rental. The following discussion should help clarify this issue.

Credit cards

Credit cards are the most frequently used method of payment. Rental companies accept the major credit cards such as Visa, MasterCard, American Express, Discover, Diners Club, Carte Blanche, and Optima. Many companies accept other credit cards as well.

Credit cards are also the preferred method of qualifying for rental. They not only provide the rental company with the best guarantee that it will be paid for the rental charges, but also they serve as an important additional form of identification.

When you arrive at the rental counter, you will be asked for your driver's license and a major credit card. The card you provide will be used to qualify you for rental. The rental agent will then swipe your card and submit a credit authorization request to the credit card company for the estimated rental charges. Some companies also add an additional amount (usually a percentage of the total rental charge, subject to state law) just in case your charges exceed the estimated amount.

Your credit card account will not actually be charged until the vehicle is returned and the rental transaction is closed. However, the amount of the credit authorization may be deducted from the available credit limit at the opening of the rental transaction. This means that you might not have that amount of credit available for other uses during the rental period.

Rental companies place this hold on the estimated rental charge to make certain that enough credit will exist when it comes time to actually pay for the rental.

Additional points to remember in regards to the use of credit cards:

- The credit card must be valid throughout the rental period.
- The card must be in the name of the individual signing the rental agreement (the renter).
- The signature on the credit card must match that on the renter's driver's license.

Debit/bank cards

There is currently a lack of uniformity in the degree to which rental companies accept debit/bank cards. Some companies will not accept a debit/bank card to qualify you for the rental but will allow you to use one in paying your bill at the close of the rental transaction. Other companies will accept a debit/bank card to qualify you but will place a hold on your funds (for the estimated rental charge) for the entire rental period. Some will accept a debit/bank card only if it does not require the input of a personal identification number (PIN).

Vouchers

Some customers prepay their rental charge as part of a travel package. It is most common with customers who have booked their entire vacation through a travel agent, including air, hotel, and rental car.

In these cases, the travel agent will provide the customer with a document known as a voucher. The voucher will include all details of the car rental, including the pickup and return dates, the vehicle class, and the inclusion of any optional protection packages.

An important point to remember is that vouchers may not include additional charges such as taxes, surcharges, refueling fees, mileage charges, additional driver fees, protection package fees, or other added costs. When purchasing a travel package, you should clarify exactly what is included with your car rental and make sure that it is clearly stated on your voucher.

Direct billing

Business customers with corporate agreements often ask the rental company to bill their business directly for rental charges. These travelers are not required to pay for each transaction.

Establishing a direct bill account typically requires a formal application and approval process as well as some degree of business volume commitment from the customer. Because direct billing requires additional administration on the part of the rental company, it is often offered only to certain levels of corporate customers.

Cash

As with debit/bank cards, rental companies will accept cash in payment of a bill at the close of the rental transaction but may not accept it as a means of qualifying for rental.

Most rental companies prefer that you qualify for rental with a major credit card. Some companies will accept a cash deposit in lieu of a credit card but only if the company has already approved you as a "cash customer."

The cash approval process usually requires the completion of an application and a credit check. Rental companies that accept cash as a deposit sometimes make this accommodation for certain customers, especially local customers who rent regularly.

ADDITIONAL DRIVERS

The preceding discussion was limited to customer qualifications that must be met by the renter. But what about when a customer wants to include additional drivers on the rental contract as authorized operators of the rental car?

First of all, the rental contract defines two classes of authorized drivers. The first class typically includes the renter, the renter's spouse, and the renter's employer, employees, and coworkers when engaged in a business-related activity. These individuals are considered authorized drivers under the terms of the rental contract.

The second class includes individuals who do not fall into the above definition but are specifically named on the rental contract as additional drivers or additional authorized drivers.

Most rental companies do not require the qualification of the first class of authorized drivers. These individuals, such as a renter's spouse, are usually not required to be present at the counter at the beginning of the rental transaction.

Individuals in the second class (those specifically named on the contract) are required to be present in order to verify that they possess a valid driver's license. They may also be subject to a driving record check. If they do meet the company's qualification standards, there is usually an additional driver fee added to the rental charge. (An additional driver fee is usually not charged for the first class of additional drivers.)

This does not mean that anyone in the first class of authorized driver doesn't have to meet certain qualifications. The rental contract requires that all drivers meet the minimum age requirement and have a valid license. Violation of these contract terms could void any protection available under the rental contract.

OTHER SITUATIONS

Rental agents are usually allowed to use some judgment and discretion in qualifying customers. For example, if a customer appeared at the rental counter in what appeared to be an intoxicated state, the rental agent should refuse to provide a vehicle. No rental company wants to put a driver who is under the influence behind the wheel. The same would hold true for a customer who was falling asleep at the counter because of fatigue.

In these situations, a manager is often called in to assist in making the decision. If the manager agrees that the customer should not be driving at that time, the rental company will often try to arrange for some alternative means of transportation.

With all of these various methods of qualifying rental customers, there is some variation among the car rental companies. In addition, the policies of all companies tend to change from time to time. Customers having questions about a rental company's qualification process should check with that company prior to the vehicle pickup date.

chapter three

Rental Counter Confusion

Most car rental customers would agree that the vehicle pickup process can be a rather frustrating, if not stressful, experience. You were conscientious enough to make an advance reservation weeks earlier and even shopped around for the best rate. Now, after a long flight, you simply want to get through the rental process as quickly as possible, pick up your car, and be on your way.

No such luck. While the rental agent is banging away at the keyboard, he or she suddenly starts bombarding you with questions for which you really weren't prepared. Are you sure you don't want a larger (or more luxurious or sportier) vehicle? Will you be filling up the gas tank before you return the car, or do you want to pay for gas in advance? Do you need protection against damage to the rental car? Do you want the extra liability coverage?

Whenever a customer satisfaction study of the car rental industry is performed, a recurring complaint concerns the perceived "high-pressure" sales tactics used by rental agents. Although the amount of pressure varies by company and sometimes even by location within the same company, efforts to "upsell" the customer are common. Your best course of action in dealing with these sales efforts is to do your homework before you pick up your car and be prepared with your responses.

The upsell process itself is not unique to the car rental business. When you order a sandwich at a fast food restaurant, don't they ask whether you also want fries and a drink? When you purchase an appliance, don't they try to sell you on the benefits of an extended warranty? When you buy a new car, don't they try to persuade you to add expensive optional equipment?

It is a well-established sales principle that an individual is most susceptible to such upsell efforts immediately after making the basic purchase decision. That's exactly what the rental agent is trying to do. So why is the rental industry criticized for this tactic when other businesses are not? Several reasons:

- Unlike other purchase decisions, many people simply do not have an adequate understanding of the options they are being offered at the car rental counter.
- There are too many different types of options offered.
- The customer feels pressured to make these important decisions in a very short period of time.

When done right, the sales presentation of the rental agent should be consultative in nature. The agent should be trained to ask a few simple questions to help determine your needs, and then he or she should suggest some relevant options that might best suit those needs. You should then come away with the feeling that the agent's role was to guide you into making the right choices that will lead to a pleasurable rental experience.

When the pressure is turned up too high, you feel that the agent is not concerned with your comfort and well-being but is instead being driven by the amount of commission he or she will make depending on what you buy. When this happens, you leave the rental counter with a bad taste regardless of the quality of your rental experience that follows.

Some customers believe that rental companies are simply out to gouge them. All companies do rely heavily on the incremental revenue from upsells and optional product sales. But the fact remains that no company would survive without significant repeat business that comes only from having satisfied customers. No rental company wants to force you to use the competition the next time you rent. Making a few extra dollars on a single transaction and losing a customer is not a smart business decision.

Then why does it feel that the rental agent is pressuring you into accepting optional products and services? Consider the following:

- Upsells and ancillary product sales are big business and are often critical to the profitability (and sometimes survival) of the company.

Considerable resources are spent training rental agents in additional sales for this reason.

- Rental agents usually receive financial incentives for upsells and ancillary product sales. With some companies, sales incentives can end up representing a significant portion of the agents' total compensation. Problems occur when the agents' personal compensation begins to take precedence over their desire to provide advice and service to the customer.

Most rental agents do want to help you have a positive rental experience. They know you're not going to have a pleasurable vacation if you spend a week driving around with three kids crammed in the back seat of a subcompact car. If you've reserved a subcompact, they'll suggest a full-sized car or a minivan. If you don't have any insurance, they'll suggest that you purchase the coverage the company offers rather than risk personal financial consequences. They know that a year from now when you're making your next vacation reservation, you're more likely to remember the quality of your experience than the extra $5.00 or $10.00 per day you spent.

In a perfect world, rental agents would be well trained and prepared to provide the expert guidance many customers need. They would be able to quickly identify your situation at the counter and make recommendations that were in your best interests. You would thoroughly enjoy your rental experience and realize that it would not have been so pleasant if not for the agent's suggestions and advice. If you were unfortunate enough to have an accident, you would thank the agent for suggesting that you purchase optional protection from the company. You would be happy, the rental company would get its incremental revenue, and the agent would receive commission.

Unfortunately, that's not how it usually works. Despite the best training efforts of the rental companies, many rental agents aren't much more knowledgeable than the customer about some of these issues. In some companies, the new agent turnover rate is quite high. Those agents that survive usually do so only after quickly learning that the only way to make money is by pushing incremental sales to gain commissions and incentives.

So this means that you're often on your own in making these decisions at the rental counter. On occasion, you may receive superior service and the type of assistance you need. Many agents do work hard to provide you with the best possible service and advice, even if it is at the expense of a smaller paycheck. Unfortunately, the difficulty lies in determining which ones are providing sound advice and which are simply trying to drive sales.

31

The best way to deal with your confusion at the counter is to become a knowledgeable consumer. You must understand your needs before the rental agent starts peppering you with options. You need to be able to quickly say "no" to options that you don't need and focus on those you do. You need to take control of the conversation and not allow yourself to be steered in a direction you don't want to go.

Some customers believe that they are taking control by simply saying "no" to everything the rental agent suggests. That's fine if you really don't need anything. But what if you would be more comfortable in a different type of vehicle? What if you really do need some optional protection? Simply saying "no" could prove to be to your detriment.

The following discussion will focus on the issues most likely to be raised when you get to the rental counter. Not so coincidentally, they are the same issues that can quickly increase your total cost if you're not careful.

Companies typically concentrate their counter sales efforts on the following areas:
- Vehicle upsells
- Fuel options
- Other additional equipment
- Optional protection packages

VEHICLE UPSELLS

We should first explain what is meant by the term "upsell." A vehicle upsell refers to the tactic that rental agents use to convince the customer to choose a more costly rental vehicle than the one originally reserved. The obvious motivation is to generate more revenue for the rental company because the customer will pay a higher rental rate. In contrast, the term "upgrade" is generally used when the rental company offers to provide the customer with a more costly rental vehicle at no additional charge. This usually occurs when the rental company does not have the vehicle reserved available or is trying to manage its fleet inventory.

Some customers (especially infrequent renters) tend to focus solely on price when making a car rental reservation. Sometimes, when cost becomes the only factor behind their reservation decision, little or no thought is given to whether the vehicle will be adequate for their needs.

The first thing experienced rental agents will do is "size you up" to determine whether you are a good upsell candidate. In doing so, the agent may casually ask some of the questions listed below. The vehicle recommendation will be based on your answers as well as any other observations about your situation.

As a general rule, your choice of vehicle should not be where you should try to save money, especially at the expense of your safety or comfort. When a rental agent suggests a different type of vehicle, listen closely to what is said, and then evaluate whether the recommendation makes sense.

The questions you should ask yourself before finalizing your vehicle selection include:

Passenger comfort and safety requirements
- How many passengers do I have?
- Can they fit comfortably in the vehicle? (Be aware that rental contracts often include a specific provision stipulating that the number of occupants will not exceed the manufacturer's recommended capacity or possibly even the number of seat belts installed in the vehicle.)
- Is a two-door or four-door vehicle more practical?
- Do I or my passengers smoke? (Many companies now offer no-smoking vehicles at no additional charge.)

Luggage space requirements
- How many pieces of luggage will I have?
- Will the luggage fit easily in the vehicle's trunk (or storage compartment in the case of a minivan)? Luggage, packages, or other property left on the rear seat and in view are an invitation to theft.
- Will I need to transport anything else during my trip (i.e., golf clubs, ski equipment, etc.)?
- Will I need extra storage space for purchases I might make during my trip?

Purpose of trip
- How much time do I plan to spend in the vehicle during my trip?
- Will I be driving long or short distances?
- If I will be entertaining business clients, what type of impression do I want to give them?

Again, cost should become a factor only after giving proper consideration to safety and comfort-related concerns.

CAR CLASSIFICATIONS

After you determine your passenger and luggage space requirements and evaluate your other vehicle needs, you have to be able to translate the terminology used by rental companies to describe their various vehicle classifications.

Rental companies do not ask whether you want a specific make and model when you make a reservation. Instead, they refer to their own vehicle classification system. For example, they might ask whether you want a full-size vehicle. The problem is that you might not be sure exactly what is meant by "full size." How can you be? Even the rental companies often don't even agree in regards to classifications. What may be a "midsize" car with one company is an "intermediate" with another company and a "standard" with still another.

The number of car classifications used by a specific rental company can range from a half-dozen to nearly three times that number. Some of the most used classifications include:

- Economy/subcompact/compact
- Intermediate/midsize/standard
- Full size/premium/luxury
- Sports utility/full-size sports utility
- Conversion van/minivan
- Pickup
- Convertible

To complicate matters, companies sometimes break down their classifications even further, for example, full-size two-door, full-size four-door, etc. The result is that it becomes virtually impossible to understand these classification systems.

What should a customer do? The best advice is to avoid the rental company's classification game. When the agent suggests a midsize car, ask for specific examples of the makes and models that fall into that category. Then make your selection on the basis of your knowledge of the various models, not on the company's classification system.

Keep in mind that you will usually not be able to reserve a specific vehicle make and model, but you will have a better idea of the two or three vehicles you might end up with by reserving a certain class.

A few additional vehicle selection tips:

- Although there may be some differences in the equipment available on different vehicles and models, most now include air conditioning, automatic transmission, and an AM/FM stereo radio as standard equipment. But just to be safe, ask the rental agent whether the vehicle includes options that are important to you.
- Most rental vehicles come equipped with basic safety equipment including air bags, antilock brakes (ABS), and child safety locks.
- If you're planning to buy a new car in the near future, rent a model in which you may have interest. It's a good way to obtain an extended "test drive."
- Renting a car also provides you with the perfect opportunity to experience vehicles that you don't normally have the chance to drive. Is this the time to splurge and spend a few dollars more on a luxury vehicle or that convertible you've always longed for?
- Some renters recommend reserving the company's least expensive vehicle with the hope that the rental company will not have that vehicle available and will upgrade them to a more expensive model at no additional cost. If the reserved vehicle is available, these renters then ask to be upgraded and are simply charged the higher price (which they would have paid anyway had they reserved the vehicle they wanted in the first place). Although this tactic may sometimes work, there is the risk that the company might not have the vehicle you really want available for you to upgrade to, and you may get struck with the economy model you reserved.

FUEL OPTIONS

Another decision you'll be asked to make at the rental counter concerns your selection of fuel purchase options. When you pick up your rental vehicle, it has a full tank of gasoline, and the rental company requires that you return it in the same condition. If you fail to do so, you are responsible for the fuel shortage and will be billed.

Rental companies used to simply bill you for the amount of fuel required to refill the vehicle's tank. Then they creatively came up with several refueling options from which the customer could choose. Of course, the whole refueling option plan was designed to make more money for the rental companies.

Allowing for minor variances among companies, the most common fuel options include:

- **Return the vehicle with a full gas tank.** By refueling the vehicle immediately before returning it and paying for the fuel yourself, there is no additional fuel charge by the rental company. Although this is the option that makes the most economic sense from the customer's perspective, it is probably the one least used. Most rental customers, especially those on a tight schedule, do not want to take the time to stop for gasoline on their way to returning the vehicle.

- **Return the vehicle with less than a full tank.** The company will then charge you a fee for the amount of gas required to fill the tank. The per-gallon rate charged by the company will usually be somewhat higher than the average pump price at local gas stations. The higher rate reflects a service charge for the company's labor cost to have the car refueled. This may be the most common option actually used. Many rental customers really do intend to fill up the tank just before returning the car, but they simply don't get around to it. The result is that they pay a premium for the refueling.

- **Prepay the rental company for a full tank of gas.** The charge is usually comparable to the local full-service price. You then return the vehicle as close to empty as you can. You will not be credited for any unused fuel. Any fuel left in the tank (and there will always be some) becomes a bonus for the rental company.

The best option is to refuel before you return the car. By fueling up yourself (especially at a lower self-service rate), you can save a few dollars. But remember that if you don't have enough time or are unable to stop for fuel before returning the car, you'll have to "bite the bullet" and pay the rental company's inflated rate.

You should never, ever pay the company in advance for a full tank of gas. Unless you are extremely proficient at planning your trip and calculating your anticipated mileage, it is almost impossible to return the car with its gas tank close to empty. Paying in advance and returning the car with half of a tank left means that you really paid twice the local full-service price.

ADDITIONAL EQUIPMENT

Realizing the potential for enhanced customer service and increased profit, rental companies also offer other ancillary products designed to meet specific needs. Among the more common products offered at an additional charge are:

- Cellular telephones
- Child safety seats
- Ski racks
- Satellite navigational system

Cellular telephones

Most rental companies offer some type of cellular telephone service for customers to rent. These phones are usually of the portable, handheld variety, although some companies also offer vehicles that are equipped with installed cell phones.

The rental of cellular phones has become a little less popular over the past few years because virtually everyone now carries a personal cell phone. Travelers having local calling plans on their personal cellular phones can avoid expensive roaming charges by renting a phone.

When renting a cellular phone, you are ultimately responsible if the phone is lost, stolen, or damaged.

Child safety seats

All states have laws requiring infants and children of certain age or size to be restrained while occupying an auto. As a result, most rental companies offer approved child safety seats for an additional fee.

Customers are allowed to use their own safety seats if they have the seats with them. Customers traveling with infants and/or children subject to these laws will be required to rent safety seats if they don't have their own.

Ski racks

In ski areas, most rental companies offer vehicles equipped with ski racks. These vehicles require an advance reservation. Customers traveling with skis must rent either a vehicle equipped with a ski rack or a vehicle large enough to accommodate the skis inside. Rental companies will not allow you to attach your own ski rack to their vehicle.

Satellite navigational systems

Some rental companies have equipped parts of their fleet with satellite navigational technology. Renters can program their destination into the equipment and receive detailed driving directions. These systems also contain other information pertaining to local points of interest such as hotels, restaurants, arenas, museums, shopping malls, etc.

INSURANCE/PROTECTION PLANS

The rental agent will also ask you whether you want to purchase any optional protection and/or insurance plans. Although there are some variations, the most common plans include:

- Loss damage waiver
- Additional liability insurance (also called supplemental liability insurance)
- Personal accident insurance
- Personal effects coverage

Depending on the company and location, there may also be other optional protection products offered. Some of those plans include emergency sickness protection, travel assistance, and Mexico travel insurance.

Although the coverage provided by these optional plans could be valuable to you as a renter, they can also be very confusing to the average rental customer. These optional protection plans will be discussed later in great detail.

SO HOW MUCH WILL MY RENTAL ACTUALLY COST?

Imagine yourself at the rental counter and you've just gone through a discussion of the above upgrades and options with the counter representative. Assume that you have accepted some of them and rejected others. The moment of truth arrives when the agent presents the rental contract for your signature and you find that the total cost is twice the daily rate you were initially quoted.

This "rental bill shock" has become a common industry criticism. Consumer advocates claim that the rental companies advertise low rates only to tack on additional charges and pressure customers into purchasing expensive options when they arrive to pick up the car. Some critics believe that the process would be much more customer friendly if the companies would advertise the ultimate cost rather than the basic, stripped-down rate.

Some rental companies have experimented with selling an all-inclusive rate at times, although with little success. The problem is that unless all companies adopt that approach, most customers are going to shop for the lowest rate and base their decision on that rate. Any company that advertises only the basic rental rate is going to end up with much of the business at the expense of companies that offer all-in-one pricing. Until consumers become more knowledgeable about car rental pricing, we'll probably continue to see only the lowest base rates advertised.

The manner in which car rental companies price their rental vehicles is not as confusing as it might seem. First, there are several principal factors that are considered in determining your rental rate:

- **Type of vehicle:** Needless to say, renting a luxury vehicle costs more than renting a subcompact car.
- **Length of rental:** Companies will usually give you a better rate if you rent the car for a longer period of time. (More on this in the discussion of weekly rates below.)
- **Day(s) of rental:** The best deals can often be found on those days of the week when business is the slowest at a particular rental location.
- **Fleet management:** Rental companies attempt to maintain a certain balance in their inventory of vehicles. If at a particular time a location is low on midsize cars but has a surplus of full-size vehicles, it may upgrade some customers who have reservations for midsize cars to full-size vehicles at the midsize rate.
- **Competition:** As in any industry, pricing is ultimately affected by competitor rates.

DAILY RATE

After taking all of these factors into consideration, the rental company arrives at its base rate (often referred to as the daily rate). This is the rate that is quoted when you call for a reservation or visit the company's Internet site. It is also the rate that is advertised exclusive of any of the various additional charges that ultimately increase your total cost.

Keep in mind that the daily rate you are quoted may be different if you call back tomorrow (or even a couple of hours later). Pricing is heavily driven by supply and demand. If you receive a quote for a rental and the company receives a lot of reservation requests during the following 24 hours for the same vehicle classification and rental period, the quoted rate will likely be higher tomorrow. It is no different than the airline industry: as the seats fill up, the prices go up.

Unfortunately, this makes it difficult to know when you can expect to find the best price. Sometimes the best rate will be available if you reserve weeks in advance. Sometimes your best deal will be found at the last minute.

In most cases, the daily rate represents a 24-hour billing cycle. Most companies use what is called a 24-hour clock in billing. This means that if you rent a car at 10:00 a.m. on Monday, you would be charged for one day (i.e., the daily rate), provided the vehicle was returned by 10:00 a.m. on Tuesday. If you keep the vehicle longer, another day would be charged for each 24-hour period until the end of the rental period.

Be aware that there are a few companies that base their billing on a calendar day basis rather than a 24-hour clock. Under the above example, a customer who picked up the vehicle at 10:00 a.m. on Monday and returned it at 10:00 a.m. on Tuesday would be charged for two days (Monday and Tuesday) even though the rental period lasted only 24 hours. When shopping for rates, you should always clarify what type of billing system the company uses. What sometimes appears to be a good deal turns out to be more costly.

Under this 24-hour clock system, what happens if a customer who rents at 10:00 a.m. on Monday returns the car at 11:00 a.m. on Tuesday? What if it is returned at 1:00 p.m. on Tuesday?

As a general rule, rental companies allow a grace period of up to one hour after the time due without additional charge. After that one-hour grace period expires, an hourly rate is often charged. However, the hourly rate is not one-twenty-fourth of the daily rate but often one-fourth or one-third of the daily rate. After you are three or four hours late, the full daily rate charge will apply.

One important point in regards to the grace period: although the rental company might not charge you when you return the car an hour late, it may charge you an additional day's rate for any other charges such as for additional equipment or optional protection plans. So you might still incur added expense if the vehicle is not returned by the required time.

Types of daily rates

The amount of the daily rate still does not tell you everything you need to know about the price of your rental. To be able to fully understand and compare your estimated rental cost, you will need to determine the type of daily rate you are being quoted.

There are several basic rate types used by rental companies. They typically base their rate on the length of the rental and/or the mileage driven during the rental period. The most common rate types are:

- **Rates based on length of rental with unlimited mileage**
  In this situation, the customer is charged only for the number of days (using the 24-hour clock) of the rental. There is no extra charge for the miles driven. This type of rate is the most commonly used and is beneficial to renters who know that they will be driving long distances during the rental period.

- **Rates based on the length of rental and the number of miles driven**
  Using this type of rate, the customer is charged for the number of days as well as the number of miles driven. The daily charge is often a little lower than the unlimited mileage rate, so this rate appeals to customers who don't expect to put many miles on the car.

- **Rates based on length of rental with a specified number of free miles**
  This rate is based on the number of days, and the customer receives a set number of "free" miles. If the vehicle is returned and the mileage cap has not been exceeded, there is no mileage charge. If the customer goes over the number of free miles, there is a charge for the number of miles over the cap.

RATES BASED ON RENTAL PERIODS

No, we're still not done in trying to understand car rental rates. Thus far, we have confined the discussion to the concept of daily rates. Rental companies also set rates based on rental periods other than a 24-hour period:

- **Weekly rental rates**
  Companies may offer a weekly rate that provides the customer with somewhat of a "discount." The weekly rate is typically less than seven times the daily rate. Customers might end up actually paying the equivalent of five or six times the daily rate. This rate is designed to give a price break to the customer who will keep the car for a full week. (The average length of rental is between three and four days.) One reason for the price break is that the longer the rental period, the less cost the rental company incurs for vehicle cleaning, servicing, and fleet administration.

- **Weekend rates**

  Weekend rates are usually found at locations with a high concentration of Monday through Friday business rentals. Rather than having the fleet remain idle over the weekend, rental companies sometimes offer reduced rates to encourage local rentals.

OTHER RENTAL RATES

Finally, there are also some other types of rental rates used in special situations. They are usually not offered at all times and apply only under certain conditions. The most common types of "special" rates include:

- **Promotional rates**

  Rental companies sometimes offer special rates in conjunction with a marketing promotion. The special promotion may relate to a certain type of rental, vehicle, or geographic area. The rates you see advertised on television or in the newspapers are typically promotional rates. These rates usually begin and end on specific dates and are intended to generate additional business during that period.

- **One-way rental rates**

  Customers sometimes need to rent a car at one location and drop it off at another. The drop-off location may be in the next state or across the country. When this need arises, the rental company may charge a one-way rental rate that is higher than the standard rate. The extra charge reflects the additional cost incurred by the rental company in returning the vehicle to the original location.

- **"Fleet migration" rates**

  In response to seasonal business volume, national car rental companies reposition their vehicle fleets twice a year. In the late fall, a portion of the fleet is moved to the warmer southern climates such as Florida and Arizona in readiness for the winter vacationers. At the end of the winter vacation period, the companies then move these vehicles back north in preparation for the summer months. Companies often offer attractive rates to customers interested in a one-way rental during these periods. The customer gets a good rate, and the rental company gets its vehicle repositioned.

- **Flexible rates**

  Rental agents sometimes have the authority to exercise some ability to offer a discounted rate in certain situations. If the rental location's fleet is out of balance, the company might offer a special rate to convince a customer to take a different vehicle than the one reserved. Sometimes a competitor's special promotion will cause a company to match the competitor's rate. You should never assume that the rate you are given is cast in stone. It doesn't hurt to ask for a better deal. You might be surprised at the result.

OTHER RENTAL CHARGES AND FEES

After finally determining the daily rate you will be paying, you must now consider all other applicable rental charges and fees before you can arrive at your "bottom line," or your total cost of rental. Some of these additional charges may surprise you if you are not expecting them. But even if you do expect them, they may well put you into a state of shock once you start adding them up.

Some of the other charges and fees you could face when renting include:

- **Mileage fees**
  If your daily rate does not include unlimited mileage or has a mileage cap that you exceed, you will be charged an additional fee based on a per mile charge for all excess mileage.

- **Additional driver fees**
  If you add any additional drivers to your rental contract, you may be charged an additional driver fee for each individual added. Rental companies usually do not charge an additional driver fee for individuals defined as authorized drivers under the terms of the contract (such as a spouse and coworkers). But anyone else who is specifically added to the front of the contract by name will be subject to this charge.

- **Underage driver charge**
  If the rental company allows drivers under the age of 25 to operate the rental vehicle, those underage drivers are typically charged an additional fee.

- **Drop charges**
  Rental companies sometimes charge an additional fee when a vehicle is returned at a location other than where it was picked up. This fee is common in one-way rental situations. Some companies may not charge a fee but instead include it in the one-way rate.

TAXES AND OTHER FEES

One last category of expenses is going to significantly affect your total cost. This expense is not optional, so you won't even have the opportunity to decline it. Rental companies rarely mention it unless you first raise the subject. We're talking about the taxes and other fees that are levied on the company by various governmental agencies and ultimately passed on to you as the consumer.

The type and amount of fees you face will depend on where you are renting the car. These fees vary by location, but the one thing you can be sure of is that they can significantly increase your bill. Some studies estimate that these taxes and fees alone can increase your daily rate by 30% to 70%.

Although there are numerous governing bodies around the country responsible for imposing these fees, they typically fall into one of the following categories:

- Sales taxes
- Airport taxes
- Airport concession fees
- Vehicle registration and licensing fees
- Special project surcharges

You would expect to have to pay certain sales taxes, just as you would for other products and services. The airport concession fees and vehicle licensing fees are somewhat controversial because they relate to costs incurred by the rental companies and passed on to the customer. Some critics feel that these fees should be borne by the rental companies as a cost of doing business. However, it that were to happen, the expense would probably still find its way to the customer in the form of higher rental rates.

The special project surcharges are a somewhat recent development. They are usually collected to help fund a special project such as a convention center or a sports arena. One theory is that state and local legislatures tag these fees onto such items as rental cars and hotel rooms in order to avoid having local residents carry the financial load. Better to target the out-of-state travelers who can't vote them out of office.

DISCOUNTS

Before you're done at the rental counter, be sure to ask the agent whether you might be entitled to any discounts. Many rental companies offer discounts to members of organizations such as the American Automobile Association

(AAA), the American Association of Retired Persons (AARP), the Small Business Association (SBA), and others. If you have membership in any organization, trade association, or club, it doesn't hurt to ask whether a discount might be available.

YOUR FINAL COST

You've finally reached the point where you can calculate your total rental cost. To do so, you need to not only determine your daily rate but also understand how it will be calculated. Remember, it might not necessarily be the rate you were initially quoted if you decided to take a different vehicle than the type you reserved.

Next, you must add in any fees or charges for additional or underage drivers, fuel options, additional equipment, and optional protection. Finally, you determine the extent of taxes and fees that will apply.

You may find that your final cost is several times higher than the basic rate you were quoted. This is exactly the reason that rental companies shy away from mentioning any of these additional charges, fees, and taxes until you appear to pick up your car.

The best way to control these runaway costs is to be an educated renter. Know exactly what you need before you get to the counter and have your responses ready when the questions start coming at you. Only by being fully prepared can you avoid making the mistake of paying unnecessary charges for equipment and services you don't need.

chapter four

The Rental Contract in Plain Terms

To effectively set forth the relationship of both parties to the rental transaction, some type of formal agreement is needed. The agreement used for this purpose in the car rental industry is referred to as the rental contract, or rental agreement.

The rental contract is a legal contract between the rental company and rental customer intended to clearly describe the duties and responsibilities of each party. This is done by means of the terms and conditions contained in the contract.

The rental contract is considered a contract of adhesion. This means that the terms of the agreement were drafted by one party without the other party having any input or opportunity to negotiate those terms. In the rental industry, the contract is written by the rental company and offered to the customer on a "take it or leave it" basis.

Under a contract of adhesion, courts typically rule in favor of the party that did not write the contract when an ambiguity exists. In a car rental situation, an ambiguity would probably be decided in favor of the customer. For that reason, rental companies are very careful in the manner in which they draft their rental contracts. This may explain why the rental contract is so difficult to read and understand. The rental company feels the need to include certain terms and conditions in order to adequately protect itself.

Most customers have little idea what is contained in the rental contract. Few ever take the time to read even parts of it. The contract is set in front of you at the counter, and you proceed to sign it so you can be on your way.

Some renters believe that as long as they have insurance, they are adequately protected against any potential financial risk. But effectively managing your financial risk involves much more than that. It is also necessary that you understand the terms and conditions of the rental contract because violation of certain provisions can not only void any protection you may have but also may create additional exposures.

Although all of the terms and conditions of the rental contract are important and included for a reason, some provisions are more important than others in terms of their potential financial impact on you. The discussion that follows will give special emphasis to those sections of the contract.

The rental contracts used by the various companies differ to some degree, but there are some standard provisions that are generally found in each. The only question then becomes where they are located in each agreement and whether there is any variance in these terms and conditions.

Any discussion of rental contract provisions must be somewhat general in nature. When renting a car, you should not fully rely on the information that follows but instead rely on the actual provisions of your rental contract. This information is intended to simply help you understand what provisions are important and what they mean to you.

FRONT OF THE RENTAL CONTRACT

The front of the rental contract contains some basic information about the rental transaction that can be categorized as follows:

- Information about the renter
- Information about the rental transaction
- Renter's selection of optional equipment and services
- Rental charges
- Renter's signature

Information about the renter

Depending on the rental contract form used by the rental company, the front of the contract may include the following information:

- **Renter's name:** The individual listed on the rental contract as the renter is the person fully responsible for the rental vehicle and its operation. The renter is also the person required to sign the rental contract.
- **Renter's address:** This information is often taken from your driver's license. If the address on your license is not current, you should inform the agent of your correct address.
- **Renter's telephone number:** The rental company wants your current telephone number in case it needs to contact you for any reason at a later date (i.e., billing problem, accident investigation, etc.).
- **Renter's date of birth:** This information is checked to verify that you meet the rental company's minimum age requirement.
- **Renter's driver's license number:** The state of issuance and expiration date may also be listed on the contract.
- **Renter's employer:** You may be asked to provide your employer's name, especially if the rental is made under a corporate agreement your company has with the rental company. You may also be asked for your business telephone number as another means of contacting you.
- **Local telephone number:** The rental company may also want to know where you can be contacted during the rental period.

Information about the rental transaction

The front of the contract may also contain the following information about the rental transaction:

- **Rental contract number:** Every rental contract includes a number, assigned by the rental company, that will be used to identify your rental transaction. In the event you need to contact the rental company for any reason during your rental period, you should provide your contract number for identification purposes.
- **Rental location:** The address or location of the rental facility where the vehicle is picked up will be listed.
- **Rental time:** The contract will list the date and exact time the contract was opened.
- **Return location:** The location of the rental facility where the vehicle will be returned at the end of the rental period may also be included.

- **Return time:** The contract may indicate the date and time the vehicle is due to be returned. This field is usually left blank until the vehicle is actually returned, and then that date and time are shown.
- **Vehicle make and model:** The make and model of the rental vehicle will be listed. The contract may also identify the vehicle classification, often in the form of a rental company code.
- **Vehicle identification number:** The contract will indicate the vehicle identification number (known as the VIN) to identify the specific rental vehicle.
- **Vehicle license plate number:** The license plate number (with the state of issuance) may also be listed as identification.
- **Vehicle mileage:** The current mileage on the vehicle is shown on the contract and is used to calculate the total mileage put on the vehicle during the rental period.
- **Additional drivers:** If the renter chooses to add any additional drivers to the rental contract, they will be listed (by name) on the front of the contract.
- **Additional driver information:** The contract may also require information about all additional drivers (address, telephone, date of birth, driver's license number).

Renter's selection of optional equipment and services
The front of the rental contract will indicate the renter's selections (if any) in regards to:
- Vehicle upgrades
- Fuel options
- Additional equipment
- Optional protection plans

For the optional protection plans, the contract usually includes an area in which the renter is required to initial either acceptance or rejection. For the fuel purchase and other options, the renter may also be required to initial his or her acceptance.

Rental charges
The front of the contract provides an itemization of rental charges including the basic rate, surcharges, fees for optional equipment and services, and taxes.

Renter's signature

The renter is required to sign the rental contract (usually at the bottom of the front side) before receiving the keys to the rental vehicle. Some companies require additional drivers added to the rental contract to also sign.

By signing the contract, the renter confirms that all of the information listed on the contract is accurate. Any misrepresentation on behalf of the renter could void any protection available to the renter as part of the rental transaction.

BACK OF THE RENTAL CONTRACT

The backside of the rental contract contains the notorious "small print"—the terms and conditions so critical to the rental transaction.

There are several reasons why customers neglect to read the rental contract. Some may be in a hurry and don't want to take the time. Others may be intimidated by the fine print and legal jargon. Some simply never choose to delve into it.

Rental customers who do try to read the contract sometimes have trouble fully understanding its terms and conditions for several reasons. First, the contract seems to presuppose some understanding of the car rental business by using terms specific to the industry that are not well defined in the contract itself. Also, most contracts leave little doubt that they were drafted by attorneys whose main intent was to create an effective legal contract, not an easy-to-read document.

Rather than providing a line-by-line interpretation of the rental contract's terms and conditions, the discussion that follows will identify and explain those conditions most important to you in regards to your potential financial exposure.

As you read the information that follows, the most important point to remember is that your failure to abide by the terms of the contract could result in what the rental industry refers to as a contract violation. If you violate the contract, the rental company could refuse to honor any vehicle damage waiver or provide any liability protection you might have otherwise received, even when you paid extra to purchase that protection!

WHO CAN DRIVE THE RENTAL CAR?

The rental contract states that only individuals deemed to be authorized drivers may operate the rental car. In order to determine exactly who is considered an authorized driver, you must understand the rental contract definitions:

Renter: The person who signs the rental agreement (thus executing the rental contract with the car rental company) is considered the renter. Most rental contracts clearly identify the name of the renter on the front of the contract form. The contract also provides a space for the renter's signature at the bottom of the form.

Authorized drivers: The rental company assumes that the person named as renter will operate the vehicle and therefore considers this individual to be an authorized driver.

In addition to the renter, certain other individuals (or categories of individuals) are generally considered to be authorized drivers. Because only those individuals who specifically qualify as authorized drivers may operate the rental vehicle, it is important to pay close attention to this definition when reviewing your rental contract form.

Keeping in mind that there might be some industry variances, the term "authorized driver" is generally defined to include (in addition to the renter):

- The renter's spouse
- The renter's employer, employees, or coemployees but only while engaged in a business activity with the renter
- Other individuals specifically named as additional drivers on the front of the rental agreement

It is critical to understand that if an individual does not fit into one of the three categories listed above, he or she *should not be allowed to operate the rental vehicle!*

Some rental contracts include other categories of authorized drivers either as a result of marketing considerations or in response to specific statutory requirements. For example, a contract might also include the following individuals as classes of authorized drivers:

- Other members of the renter's immediate family who are also residents of the renter's household.
- Valet parking attendants while parking the rental vehicle at commercial establishments

51

- Other individuals in an emergency situation (For example, if the renter becomes seriously ill and is unable to drive, a passenger might qualify as an authorized driver in order to get the renter to emergency medical care.)

At one time, the definition of authorized driver was much broader in most rental contracts, with the final three categories above typically included. But in an effort to better manage their risk, many companies have whittled away at the list.

This is an area of the contract that rental companies strictly interpret. If you allow someone to operate the vehicle who is not an authorized driver, you will face a major problem if an accident occurs or the rental car becomes damaged while this person is driving.

You should always disclose to the rental agent all individuals who might be driving, especially if you are unclear whether they qualify as authorized drivers. It is always better to add a person to the contract and pay the additional driver fee than to be found in violation of the rental contract and be faced with an accident claim for which you will not receive any protection.

Rental qualifications

Simply falling into one of the above categories by definition does not alone qualify an individual as an authorized driver. In order to be considered an authorized driver of the rental vehicle under the terms of the contract, all individuals must also meet the company's rental requirements.

Every authorized driver must qualify for rental by:
- Possessing a valid driver's license
- Meeting the company's minimum age requirement
- Having an acceptable driving record

WHERE CAN YOU DRIVE THE RENTAL VEHICLE?

Rental contracts include restrictions about where the vehicle may be operated. Major rental companies usually allow their vehicles that are rented in the United States to be operated anywhere in the country as well as in Canada. Most rental contracts specifically prohibit taking the vehicle into Mexico without the expressed permission of the rental company.

Some rental contracts, especially those used by smaller regional rental companies, further restrict the "territory" in which the vehicle may be operated. Sometimes these contracts limit the territory to the actual state where the rental takes place. Others may limit usage to a geographic region that might include several states. Some take a slightly different approach by allowing the vehicle to be operated anywhere except in specifically named states. (This is usually intended to avoid operation in states having vicarious liability laws or any other factors that significantly increase the rental company's risk.)

HOW CAN YOU USE THE RENTAL VEHICLE?

The rental contract defines not only who may and may not operate the rental vehicle and where it may be operated but also how the vehicle can be used (or more importantly, how it may not be used).

Prohibited use of the rental vehicle

All rental contracts contain a list of prohibited uses. The terms of these rental contracts usually state that the use or operation of the rental vehicle in violation of any prohibited use will be considered a contract violation and could void any protection or benefits that would otherwise be available to the renter under the contract.

The list of prohibited uses will vary by rental car company and rental location but will generally include some or all of the following in requiring that the rental vehicle will not be used by anyone who:

- is not an authorized driver
- obtains the vehicle on the basis of false or misleading information
- as a result of reckless misconduct damages the vehicle or causes personal injury or property damage to another
- is intoxicated or under the influence or any substance that impairs driving ability
- uses the vehicle during the commission of a felony or for the transportation of illegal drugs or contraband
- allows more passengers to occupy the vehicle than there are seat belts or who does not require all occupants to comply with applicable seat belt and child-restraint laws
- drives the vehicle off of regularly maintained and paved roadways
- drives outside the United States and Canada
- leaves the vehicle and fails to remove the keys, close and lock all doors, windows, and the trunk or otherwise aids in vandalism or theft of the vehicle

- does not know how to operate a manual transmission (if the vehicle has a manual transmission)
- under continued operation of the vehicle is likely to cause damage to the vehicle
- engages in any speed contest
- carries people or property for hire (unless otherwise agreed by the company)
- pushes anything
- tows anything (unless the rented vehicle is equipped with towing equipment also rented from the company)
- improperly fuels the vehicle (gasoline in a diesel-powered vehicle or diesel fuel in a gasoline-powered vehicle)
- improperly loads the vehicle or transports weight exceeding the vehicle's maximum capacity
- carries hazardous or explosive substances

This list of prohibited uses is based on a compilation of those most commonly found in the rental contracts of various car rental companies. When renting a car, the list of prohibited uses that is found in your contract may differ, so you should always review the terms of your rental contract before operating the vehicle.

VEHICLE DAMAGE

The terms and conditions of the rental contract describe your responsibility for damage to the rental vehicle. They often include information about how you can avoid or minimize your vehicle damage exposure by purchasing the company's loss damage waiver (LDW) or by relying on your own insurance.

Because of the importance and complexity of this issue, your responsibility for vehicle damage and how you can effectively manage that exposure will be discussed in detail later in this text.

LIABILITY PROTECTION

The rental contract describes the liability protection that may be provided under the contract. In addition to explaining the liability protection available to you, the contract may mention that increased liability protection can be purchased.

Again, because this topic can be quite confusing and represents a huge financial exposure to you, it will be discussed later.

REFUELING OPTIONS
The company's refueling options, including your responsibilities under each, are described in the rental contract.

OTHER OPTIONAL PROTECTION
The rental contract typically lists other optional protection plans available to renters and may provide an overview of the coverage. This optional protection may include such plans as personal accident insurance (PAI) and personal effects coverage (PEC).

A review of these other optional protection plans offered by rental companies will be discussed later in this text.

OTHER RENTAL CONTRACT TERMS AND CONDITIONS
The terms and conditions of the rental contract can appear to be quite complex. Some of them are very important, such as those described above. Other provisions, while perhaps not as critical from a financial perspective, can become important to you, especially if you are not aware of them and inadvertently violate one.

Some of the more relevant provisions not yet discussed include:
- **Traffic violations and fines:** If you receive a traffic or parking ticket while operating a rental car, you are fully responsible for all fines and other costs. If you ignore a parking ticket and the rental company, as owner of the vehicle, is required to respond to it, it will hold you responsible for any resultant fines. The company may also charge you an additional administrative fee.
- **Vehicle repairs:** You cannot authorize any repairs to the vehicle without the rental company's consent. If the vehicle breaks down or has mechanical problems, you must contact the company before taking any action.
- **Condition of vehicle:** You are required to return the vehicle in the same condition as it was when you took possession of it. If you return the vehicle full of trash, the rental company may assess a cleaning charge.

- **Failure to return vehicle:** The contract may describe the action the rental company will take if you fail to return the vehicle when it is due. This action could include the filing of stolen vehicle charges and the issuance of a warrant for your arrest. The company may also bill you for its costs in seeking the recovery of its vehicle.
- **Property left in vehicle:** Renters frequently forget to remove all of their personal property from the vehicle when they turn it in. They then return to or call the rental facility looking for their sunglasses, cameras, or other such items. If the property cannot be found, the customer becomes understandably upset because no one but a rental company employee could have taken it. However, because the contract may state that the rental company is not responsible for property left in the car, the customer will have a difficult time getting any satisfaction.
- **Investigation assistance:** If your rental car is involved in an accident or other loss, you are required to fully cooperate with the rental company in its investigation and handling of the matter. This may include completing loss reports, giving statements or depositions, and other such tasks. You are also required to immediately notify the rental company and deliver any related documents you receive.
- **Payment:** The contract may state that you, as the renter, are fully responsible for the payment of all charges. This is especially relevant in the case of a business rental. If you were traveling on behalf of your employer who, for some reason, refused or was not able to pay the bill, you would be responsible as the individual who signed the contract.
- **Consequential damages:** The contract may contain a provision absolving the rental company from any liability for your failure to land a big deal because the car broke down and you missed your meeting.

WHAT WILL HAPPEN IF YOU VIOLATE THE TERMS OF THE RENTAL CONTRACT?

The consequences for violating the terms of the rental contract depend on which terms you violate. If you allow the vehicle to be operated by an unauthorized driver or if you are found to have violated a use restriction, you could be held financially responsible for any loss of or damage to the vehicle and may not be afforded any liability or other protection normally provided under the terms of the contract. In addition, any optional protection purchased from the rental company could be voided.

If you violate one of the other provisions, the consequence would probably be less severe and would depend on the circumstance (for example, being responsible for the cost of a parking ticket).

The rental contract is a legally binding agreement between you and the rental company. It describes, in detail, your obligations and responsibilities as well as those of the rental company. Just as with any contract, if you fail to live up to the terms of the contract, you may face significant repercussions.

No one finds a rental contract to make for stimulating reading. But because you are responsible for knowing what information it contains (remember that when you signed the rental contact, you confirmed that you understood and agreed with its contents), it would be in your best interest to take the time to read through one just once.

The next time you travel, take a look at your rental contract during some quiet time in your room or on an airplane. Compare the information discussed above with what you find in the contract. You'll probably find quite a few similarities and possibly some differences. The exercise should help you better understand the policies of the rental company and avoid any unpleasant surprises.

chapter five

Responsibility for Damage to the Rental Vehicle

You assume responsibility for any damage that occurs to your rental car while it is in your possession. The extent of your financial responsibility extends to the full value of the vehicle. In addition, you could find yourself faced with additional indirect costs you didn't expect.

A rental company's fleet is its most expensive physical asset—and its primary revenue-producing asset. If a company doesn't have vehicles or if its vehicles are in such poor condition that no one wants to rent them, it will not remain in business very long. Neither can it make a profit if its vehicle repair costs become unmanageable and the cars are constantly out of use while being repaired. To protect their investment, car rental companies want to make sure that customers use care in operating their cars.

The most effective way for the rental companies to accomplish this is to transfer the financial responsibility for damage to their customers. By making customers responsible for damage costs, the company hopes that renters will have enough incentive to protect the cars as if they were their own. Without that responsibility, customers would have little reason to care for their rental cars.

YOUR RESPONSIBILITY FOR LOSS OF OR DAMAGE TO THE RENTAL VEHICLE

Although most car renters do understand that they have responsibility for vehicle damage that occurs, few understand that this responsibility is not limited to damage that results from their negligent care or operation of the vehicle. Many renters believe that if another party caused the damage to the vehicle, they will not be held financially responsible.

The terms of the rental contracts used by most car rental companies contain language that holds you, as renter, financially responsible for all damage— even if it resulted from someone else's negligence. This provision states that your responsibility includes any and all damage that occurs during the rental period regardless of fault. The effect is that your responsibility for loss of or damage to the rental vehicle becomes greatly expanded and is based on the contractual liability that results when you sign the rental agreement rather than on the concept of negligence.

By entering into the rental contract, you agree to return the vehicle in the same condition as when you took possession at the start of the rental period, except for normal wear and tear. This means that regardless of how the damage occurs (with some exceptions noted below), you will be held responsible.

For example, you could be responsible for vehicle damage in the following situations:

- You are stopped at a traffic light, and another vehicle strikes your rental car in the rear.
- A car runs a red light and hits your vehicle.
- Your rental car is struck while it is legally parked and unoccupied.
- Your rental car is stolen or vandalized while properly locked.

This important point bears repeating: your financial responsibility for damage to the rental car exists *regardless of how the damage occurs*. In the above examples, you probably would have been found to be free of negligence and any legal liability for the damage. But because of your contractual agreement to return the vehicle in the same condition it was in at the start of the rental period, you assume financial responsibility.

VEHICLE DAMAGE RESPONSIBILITY EXCEPTIONS

There are some exceptions to this rule. Some car rental companies use rental contracts containing a provision stating that the renter will not be held financially responsible for damage caused by or resulting from (1) accidental fire that does not result from a collision and (2) acts of God (such as windstorms, floods, and other natural phenomena).

The intent of this language is to avoid the customer and public relations repercussions that might result from holding the renter financially responsible for damage caused by forces over which he or she clearly has no control (such as acts of God or nature).

Some companies keep this provision in their contracts, but others have quietly eliminated it for several reasons. First, renters who have personal auto insurance often find that these types of losses are covered by their policies. Providing this exception ultimately benefits the renter's insurance company more than it does the renter. Also, some companies felt that renters who knew that they would be held responsible for this type of damage might be more likely to protect the vehicle from storms and other natural causes when they had advance warning.

To determine whether any exceptions exist in regards to the extent of your responsibility for vehicle damage, you should refer to the provisions relating to damage to the vehicle, usually located on the back of your rental contract.

OTHER RESPONSIBLE PARTIES

Although you as the renter of the vehicle are ultimately responsible for any damage because of the contractual liability you assume by executing the rental contract, there are situations in which you (or your insurer) might avoid having to pay for the damage.

This typically occurs when the proximate cause of the damage is the negligence of another party. For example, let's say that you are behind the wheel of your rental car and are stopped at a traffic light, and your vehicle is struck in the rear. If the rental company can successfully recover the full amount of its damages from the party who struck you, you could be ultimately relieved of your contractual responsibility.

When one of its vehicles is damaged, a rental company is concerned with only one thing: recouping the financial loss it has sustained. It does not really care who pays the bill as long as the bill does get paid.

In fact, upon notification of a loss, most rental companies will immediately send a "subrogation notice" to any and all parties that could conceivable have responsibility for the damage. ("Subrogation" refers to the process of trying to recover one's damages from the party legally responsible for those damages.)

These parties that the rental company might pursue include:

- The renter or driver of the rental vehicle or his or her insurance companies
- The renter's credit card company
- The owner or driver of the other vehicle(s) or his or her insurance companies

When the damage was the result of the negligence of a party other than the renter, the rental company will often pursue the negligent party first, but the renter will ultimately be held responsible if the negligent party cannot or will not pay.

DETERMINING THE AMOUNT OF VEHICLE DAMAGE

If you are involved in an accident or the rental vehicle is otherwise damaged while in your possession, how will the rental company measure the amount of damage to the vehicle (often referred to as "direct damage") to determine how much to bill you?

The rental company will first determine whether the vehicle can be repaired. Under insurance industry standards, when the estimated repair cost is less than the fair market value of the vehicle minus the value of the vehicle's salvage, it is usually considered to be repairable. In a scenario involving a rental vehicle, there may also be other considerations involving "diminished value" (as discussed below).

If the vehicle is repairable, you will be asked to reimburse the rental company for its actual repair costs. This means that you should be billed at that actual repair labor rate customarily paid by the rental company. The rental company should also charge you for the actual cost of replacement parts.

Rental companies often have arrangements with auto shops that allow the company to pay discounted rates for both parts and labor. These arrangements are based on the high volume of repair work the rental company provides to the shop and are perfectly legal as long as the benefit of the discounts is passed on to any party who ultimately reimburses the rental company for the damage. In other words, the rental company can't pay "wholesale" repair rates and then turn around and bill you based on the "retail" cost.

Before agreeing to pay the amount sought by the company, you should request an itemized repair bill detailing the parts replaced (with prices) and the number of labor hours. You should also ask for a copy of the paid repair invoice or other proof that the amount of the bill was actually paid by the company.

Most major rental companies would not engage in the practice of treating vehicle repairs as a "profit center" by charging you more for repairs than they actually paid. However, this does not mean that this type of abuse never occurs. As a diligent consumer, it is your responsibility to make certain that the amount billed is accurate and reasonable. If you have personal auto physical damage insurance, this becomes the job of your insurer.

If you don't have any insurance, the best course of action is to have an auto repair shop you trust review the repair bill for accuracy. Although the repair shop will not have the benefit of inspecting the damaged vehicle, it can determine whether parts prices are correct and labor charges reasonable. If the repair documentation does not reflect discounted prices and labor rates, the amount of the bill should probably be questioned, and you should definitely ask to see proof of the rental company's payment to the shop.

TOTAL LOSSES

In accordance with the criteria it has established, a rental company may decide that its vehicle should not be repaired. The company will weigh factors such as the vehicle's current market value, the cost to repair the vehicle, and the amount that could be realized from the sale of the vehicle's salvage to determine which course of action to take. If it decides that the vehicle should not be repaired, it will be considered a "total loss."

In measuring a renter's financial responsibility for a total loss, the rental company will charge the renter for the "fair or current market value" of the vehicle minus the amount the rental company actually derives from the sale of the vehicle salvage. Some government regulators have defined "fair market value" as the vehicle's price as listed in an industry-wide and generally accepted publication or directory of used car values or the retail price received in a commercially reasonable sale.

If you find yourself responsible for the total loss of a rental vehicle, you're probably faced with a sizable amount. Before agreeing to pay the total claimed by the rental company, you should ask the company to thoroughly explain how it arrived at that amount. After doing so, you may also want to have the calculation reviewed by an attorney or other individual knowledgeable in such matters.

LOSS OF TURN-BACK VALUE

Rental car companies sometimes purchase vehicles under "repurchase" programs sponsored by vehicle manufacturers. Under these programs, the rental company agrees to purchase a specified number of vehicles with the guarantee that the manufacturer will buy the vehicles back at some point in the future at a specified predetermined price. In most cases, the arrangement benefits the rental company because the predetermined resale price is often higher than the wholesale value of the vehicles that the company would receive in the open market. In addition, the guaranteed repurchase price allows for greater financial accounting certainty and stability for the rental company.

There are often certain criteria that must be met before the manufacturer will accept the vehicle back. There is usually a mileage cap that cannot be exceeded at turn-back time. (Some arrangements allow the mileage cap to be exceeded, but the rental company then must pay a per-mile charge for mileage above the stated cap.)

Under the terms of a typical repurchase agreement, a vehicle cannot have sustained damage to its frame or body damage above a specified monetary threshold. When the extent of damage exceeds the stated threshold, the vehicle is disqualified from the program and cannot be returned to the manufacturer.

This means that the rental company will probably have to sell the vehicle at a wholesale auction and realize less from the sale than it would have under the guaranteed program. When this occurs, the rental company may want to include the difference (between the guaranteed turn-back value and the amount it actually gets) in the total claim it pursues against the renter or other responsible party.

This poses an interesting problem that is sometimes difficult for those outside the rental industry to comprehend. For the sake of simplicity, let's assume that the "damage threshold" for a $22,000 vehicle is $2,000. This means that should the vehicle sustain more than $2,000 in body damage, it is disqualified from the repurchase program (even if it is first repaired).

Let's further assume that this vehicle sustains damage totaling $4,000. Under the terms of the guaranteed repurchase program, the rental company would have received $17,000 from the manufacturer when it was sold back at a specified time. But because the vehicle has been disqualified, the rental company now is forced to sell it at auction at a price of $15,000. Under this scenario, the rental company might bill you $6,000 ($4,000 for the direct repairs *plus* $2,000 for its loss of turn-back value).

Can you legally be held responsible for the loss of turn-back value? The justification used by the rental companies is that the actual dollar loss they incur can be easily documented using the repair invoice, the vehicle sales receipt, and the repurchase agreement. The companies feel that because the loss can be clearly proven and is not based on speculation, they are entitled to compensation.

The issue of rental companies claiming or collecting loss of turn-back value from renters has been the subject of review by the Federal Trade Commission (FTC). In a 1996 order, the FTC held that if a rental company intends to seek loss of turn-back value from its renters, it must clearly and prominently disclose to renters that (1) their exposure for damage to the vehicle could exceed the actual amount of repairs or the fair market value of the vehicle and (2) if the renter's insurance company won't pay the charge, the renter will become personally responsible.

This disclosure must appear in any representation that relates to the renter's responsibility for damage to the rental vehicle including rental contracts, brochures, and automated reservation systems. The order from the FTC further stated that any demand for payment for loss of turn-back value must clearly disclose the amount of the claim attributed to loss of turn-back value and explain how it was calculated. This may appear confusing, but the important point is that the rental company might try to collect loss of turn-back value from you provided that it first makes proper disclosure of its intent to do so.

Understand that this disclosure requirement applies only to the rental company's efforts to collect from renters on the basis of their contractual relationship. When a third party is determined to be the proximate cause of damage to a rental car, the company can pursue recovery of its damages on the basis of the third party's negligence. It then becomes an issue of fact and proof of damages as to whether the negligent third party is determined to be legally liable for the rental company's full loss, including its loss of turn-back value.

Needless to say, without a contractual basis for claiming loss of turn-back value from a third party, this aspect of the company's damages becomes highly subject to negotiation. A third party's ability to resist payment may be ultimately determined by whether any applicable case law exists.

RESPONSIBILITY FOR INDIRECT DAMAGES

In addition to responsibility for direct physical loss of or damage to the rental vehicle, rental contracts may also hold the renter responsible for:

- Loss of use
- Other related administrative expenses

Loss of Use

When a rental vehicle is damaged and forced out of service, the rental company will hold the renter responsible for its resultant loss of revenue while the vehicle is being repaired or replaced. The rationale used is that the company cannot rent the vehicle in its damaged state, so it loses the ability to produce revenue and is entitled to compensation.

How does the rental company determine how much revenue it actually lost? Some type of formula is typically used to arrive at that figure. One of the more common formulas is daily rental rate x number of days out of service x average utilization rate = loss of revenue. (Average utilization rate is calculated by determining the percentage of days during the month that a vehicle is out on rent.)

For sake of illustration, assume that a vehicle rents for $40.00 per day, is out on rent 80% of the time, and is out of service for 10 days after an accident. Under this scenario, the revenue lost would be $320.00 ($40.00 x 80% x 10). The rental company would therefore add $320.00 to its claim for this loss of use.

When presented with a claim for loss of use, you should pay close attention to the number of days the car is out of service. Your responsibility should be limited to the length of time it takes to actually complete the repairs and not for any unnecessary delays caused by the repair shop or rental company. For example, you may be billed for the vehicle being out of service for 12 days, but the actual repairs took only five. You should not be responsible for the seven days that the repair shop waited for parts to arrive or didn't have enough repairmen to complete the job.

How do you determine the number of days it should have taken to perform the repairs? There is no clear formula, but as a rule of thumb, you should consider the number of labor hours shown on the repair estimate or bill. For instance, if the bill listed 32 labor hours, the repairs could have been completed in as few as four days (32 labor hours divided by eight hours per day). Although you should not consider this to be a hard and fast rule in helping determine loss of use (some companies use other formulas), it is a good starting point for your negotiations with the rental company.

If the rental car cannot be repaired and is considered a total loss, the loss of use should be based on the length of time required to determine that the vehicle will not be repaired.

You should never pay a loss of use claim without first trying to negotiate the amount down, if not out completely. One common argument is that unless the rental company had all of its cars out on rent (100% utilization) during the period the damaged vehicle was out of service, it did not actually lose any revenue because it did have other cars available to rent. The company will claim that it still had a right to rent that particular vehicle or use it for other purposes and is actually trying to mitigate its claim by reducing its amount of lost revenue by its actual utilization rate.

Before agreeing to pay any loss of use claim, require the rental company to prove to you that it did lose revenue as a result of the vehicle being out of service. Unless it can prove that it had no other vehicles of the same car class available, you should initially resist paying for loss of use. Even when the rental company does provide sufficient documentation to substantiate the amount of its claim, ask whether there is any applicable law to support its recovery efforts. Some states have laws that restrict a rental company's right to seek payment of loss of use.

Remember that the rental company is primarily interested in recovering its direct damages. Of course, it would also like to recover the full amount of its loss of use claim, but that amount is often highly negotiable.

Administrative Costs

It is also common for rental companies to include an additional fee for "administrative costs" in calculating the amount of the renter's responsibility for vehicle damage. The rationale is that the primary business of a rental company is not handling claims, and therefore, the cost of pursuing reimbursement of vehicle damage is an additional expense beyond the normal cost of doing business. As a result, that cost is often included in the company's claim.

The charge for administrative fees should reflect the rental company's actual expenses associated with its collection efforts. It should not serve as a profit center for the company. However, because attempting to itemize the actual expenses can obviously be quite burdensome, most companies will instead assess either a flat fee intended to represent average costs or a scaled fee based on the amount of vehicle damage.

If itemized, the actual administrative costs incurred by the rental company might include the following:

- Rental company employee time spent completing the accident or damage report
- Photographs of the damage
- Damage appraisal fees
- Cost of obtaining police reports
- Time spent delivering the vehicle for repairs and picking up after repairs
- Cost of pursuing collection (including employee time, letters, postage, copying, phone calls)
- Cost of maintaining accounting records (including processing of payments)

At first glance, it might appear that these expenses should be considered to be a cost of doing business because rental companies should expect a certain number of their vehicles to be involved in accidents and be damaged at some point. But the companies argue that if these costs were not charged to those renters responsible for vehicle damage, they would probably end up being allocated among all customers, thus increasing the cost of renting a car for everyone.

At the present time, only one state (Wisconsin) specifically prohibits the inclusion of such fees. Although a rental company's right to charge for administrative fees is established by statute in a few states, the laws of most states are silent on this issue. This is important because the absence of any legal authority establishing a rental company's right to such costs makes this aspect of the claimed amount of damages negotiable. It is often possible to convince the rental company to agree to waive the administrative fee in exchange for prompt payment of the actual direct vehicle damages.

RECEIVING A NOTICE OF A VEHICLE DAMAGE CLAIM

What should you do if a rental car is damaged while in your possession and the company sends you a recovery or subrogation notice?

If you have personal auto insurance that you believe will cover the loss, you should immediately forward the notice to your insurance company. You should also respond to the rental company by informing it of the identity of your insurer (including policy number, agent's name, and claim office address and phone number, if known. It is *not* necessary to provide any additional information.)

If you used a credit card that provides coverage for rental vehicles, contact the card company to determine its claim filing procedure. Again, you should also inform the rental company of the existence of credit card coverage.

Be aware that even if you have personal auto insurance or credit card coverage, you might not be totally relieved of your responsibility. In the event that your insurance carrier or credit card company refuses to pay any portion of the rental company's claim (such as loss of turn-back, loss of use, or administrative charges), the rental company will probably pursue you directly for the unpaid balance.

WHAT IF YOU DON'T HAVE ANY INSURANCE OR CREDIT CARD COVERAGE?

If you don't have any coverage for damage to the rental vehicle, you should still respond to the rental company's subrogation notice. Unfortunately, the lack of coverage does not free you of your responsibility, and the rental company will then ask how you plan to pay for the damage. In responding, consider the following:

- The rental company's preference is for you to make immediate payment for its full claimed amount, including loss of use and administrative fees. Before agreeing to do so, you need to understand that the rental company is always prepared to compromise (even when it indicates that it is not). You should immediately let the rental company know that before you are willing to discuss payment of its claim for direct damages, you want the loss of use and administrative fees waived.

- In discussing settlement of the direct vehicle damages, it could be worthwhile to offer the rental company the option of either a "discounted" lump sum payment or payment of the full amount over an extended installment period. The company may consider the discounted immediate payment rather than installments.

- If you don't have the financial capability to make a lump sum payment, the rental company will accept an installment payment plan. It is possible that the company might perform a check of available public records (known as an asset check) to determine your ability to pay before suggesting installment terms. Before you sign any installment agreement or promissory note, you should have the document reviewed by an attorney.

- The rental company may try to charge interest with an installment plan. Interest is usually subject to negotiation and can often be avoided. If the company insists on charging interest, you should make certain that it is legal to do so in your state.

WHAT IF YOU SIMPLY REFUSE TO PAY?

Simply ignoring a rental company's subrogation demand or refusing to pay its claim won't work. Rarely do rental companies simply walk away from these potential recoveries, especially if the amount is significant.

The rental company will probably make several attempts over a period of 90 days or so to collect the amount owed directly from you. If unsuccessful at that time, it may decide to refer the matter to an outside collection agency. Doing so will ultimately reduce the company's net recovery because the collection agency is paid a contingency fee based on the amount it collects. However, the rental company would rather concentrate on its newer claims and "easier" collections for cash flow purposes and let outside vendors work with the more difficult ones.

If the outside collection agency has difficulty collecting, it will at some point ask the rental company whether it wants to file a lawsuit or simply drop the matter. Because most attorneys who handle this type of litigation also charge on a contingency fee basis, the rental company will usually proceed with the suit provided that the amount owed warrants further effort and there is some recovery potential.

Some renters mistakenly believe that the rental company will decide that it is not practical to pursue small claims (for example, under $1,500) and will simply forget about them. On the contrary, these small claims are often vigorously pursued directly by the rental company in small claims court without the necessity of outside attorney expense.

Remember that the rental company is mainly focused on its net recovery. It is better off accepting your offer of 75% of its claim than hiring an attorney at a 33% contingency fee and collecting 100%. Keep these costs in mind when negotiating possible settlement.

WHAT IF YOU ARE CHARGED FOR DAMAGE THAT DIDN'T HAPPEN WHILE YOU HAD THE CAR?

Rental operations typically run on very thin margins. As a result, the difference between profit and loss can be dependent on "little things," such as the company's effectiveness in detecting damage to its vehicles in pursuing recovery from the responsible renter.

Ideally, rental companies want to visually inspect each vehicle for damage each time it goes out on rental and when it returns. When damage is discovered on a returning vehicle, prompt detection allows the rental agent to obtain a damage report from the renter, thus starting the collection process.

Unfortunately, vehicles might not always be inspected immediately upon return, especially during busy periods and at understaffed locations. In addition, it is sometimes difficult to spot minor damage when the inspection is performed hastily or at night. With the increasing emphasis on speeding up the rental process, the renter is sometimes already out of the lot before anyone has a chance to look at the car.

When damage is later discovered, the rental company often bills the last renter who had the car. Unfortunately, sometimes the last renter is not the one who caused the damage. It then becomes difficult for the renter to argue that the damage was preexisting.

You can avoid this type of unpleasant situation by following some simple advice. Each time you rent a vehicle, you should thoroughly inspect it personally before driving from the rental lot. If any damage is found, it should immediately be brought to the attention of a rental agent. You should also insist that the agent properly note the existence of the damage on the rental contract (both the company and customer copies). Although this inspection might take a few extra minutes, it could be well worth the time in the event that damage is discovered when the vehicle is returned. In the absence of such documentation that the damage was preexisting, you could be held responsible.

chapter six

Your Legal Liability to Others

In addition to your financial responsibility for damage to the rental vehicle, you could also find yourself legally liable for bodily injury and property damage to others that result from your use or operation of the rental vehicle.

YOUR LEGAL LIABILITY

If you are found legally liable for an accident with your rental car that causes bodily injury and/or property damage to others (referred to as third parties), you could be held financially responsible for that injury or damage. But what does it mean to be "legally liable"?

Your legal liability is determined through a review the facts of the accident in view of applicable law. A renter (or other authorized driver) who fails to exercise the degree of care required by the circumstances and defined by law is said to be "negligent" and thus legally liable, at least to some degree.

Black's Law Dictionary defines negligence as "the failure to use such care as a reasonably prudent and careful person would use under similar circumstances. The law of negligence is founded on reasonable conduct or reasonable care under all circumstances of particular case. Doctrine of negligence rests on duty of every person to exercise due care in his conduct toward others from which injury may result."

Being found negligent (and legally liable) for damages resulting from an accident does not require intent or gross recklessness. Most of the time, accidents are simply the result of a renter's inattention, poor judgment, or simply careless driving.

EXAMPLES OF NEGLIGENCE

Some examples of the careless operation of a rental car that could result in your legal liability to others include:

- Driving at an unsafe speed
- Failing to obey a traffic signal
- Following too closely behind another vehicle
- Making an improper turn
- Backing the vehicle without first making sure the way is clear
- Failing to remain in the proper lane of traffic
- Passing another vehicle when it is unsafe to do so

It is not necessary to be totally at fault for an accident to be held legally liable and face potential financial responsibility. If it is determined that both involved parties are negligent to some degree, they may share fault for the accident. Depending on the statutes and established case law that apply to the specific case, a driver could be held responsible even if found only minimally negligent.

DAMAGES

If you are involved in an accident and found legally liable, you could face financial responsibility for several types of damages:

- **Bodily injury:** Physical injury, sickness, or death that results from an accident. A person who suffers bodily injury as a result of an accident is generally entitled to monetary compensation for medical expenses, loss of earnings, and pain and suffering. Bodily injury claimants might include occupants of other vehicles, pedestrians, or even passengers occupying the rental vehicle.
- **Property damage:** Physical damage to or destruction of property, including loss of use resulting from that damage or destruction. Property damage claims might include damage to other vehicles, buildings, or other structures or property.

CONTRACTUAL VS. LEGAL LIABILITY

There is a distinct difference between your responsibility for damage to the rental vehicle and your legal liability for third-party bodily injury and property damage claims.

Your responsibility for vehicle damage is contractual and based on the terms of your signed rental contract. These contract terms hold you responsible for the loss of or damage to the vehicle regardless of fault. You can be held financially responsible even if the damage was totally the result of another party's negligence. Even if you are totally free of any degree of negligence, you remain responsible for the vehicle damage because of the provisions contained in the rental contract.

Your legal liability to others is not contractual but is instead based on tort law. A tort action must contain the following elements:

- The existence of a legal duty
- A breach of that duty
- Damages that result from that breach of duty

In the context of operating a rental car, you owe a duty to others to do so in a safe manner. If you breach that duty by failing to drive safely and your actions cause an accident, you are responsible for any injuries or damage that result.

POSSIBLE FINANCIAL IMPLICATIONS OF YOUR LEGAL LIABILITY TO OTHERS

Although your financial exposure for damage to the rental car can be significant, it is generally limited to the value of the car. Although being financially responsible for $30,000, $40,000, or more is not insignificant, it cannot compare to your potential exposure related to liability claims.

A claim made by a seriously injured third party could be worth millions of dollars. If you did not have adequate insurance to satisfy a serious claim such as this, you could become personally liable for any portion not covered by your available liability coverage. For this reason, it is extremely important to make sure you have sufficient liability coverage available while operating a rental car.

INCREASED RISK WHILE OPERATING A RENTAL CAR

Your potential legal liability arising from your operation of a rental car is not much different than the risk you face while driving your own personal vehicle. You have the same duty to operate the car in a safe manner and will be held responsible for accidents in which your negligence is determined to be a contributing factor.

Whatever your odds are of being involved in an accident while driving your own auto, they are probably greater while driving a rental car. There are several reasons:

- You may be less familiar with the operation of the rental car than you are with your personal auto. The instrument panel controls are in different places and may work differently. There may be differences in the manner in which the car steers and performs. The vehicle may be of a different size and weight. It often takes you a while to get used to your rental car.
- You may be driving in areas unfamiliar to you. Whether you are renting for business or while on vacation, you might be driving in some areas that are strange to you. Being unfamiliar with your surroundings could be distracting.
- If you're traveling on business, you may be rushing to arrive at an appointment or thinking about your business instead of paying attention to your driving.
- When on vacation, you may become a little too relaxed, which could also result in you becoming less attentive than you should be.

Your potential legal liability should not be ignored or underestimated. Being responsible for an accident and finding yourself inadequately protected by insurance could cause serious financial repercussions for you or, if traveling on business, your company.

chapter seven

Protection Provided by the Rental Company

One significant change in the car rental industry over the past decade or so is the amount of liability protection provided to you under the terms of the rental contract. At one time, rental companies provided customers with relatively high limits of primary liability protection under the provisions of the standard rental contract. This liability protection was gradually scaled back to the point where today most renters receive either only secondary liability protection or a low limit of primary protection.

This action has had two effects on the customer. The rental customer receives much less protection (if any at all) from the rental company than in the past. But it has also caused much confusion. Today, most customers have little idea about their sources of liability protection or whether they're even protected at all.

Unfortunately, there is no formula to follow in sorting through the liability issue. A renter cannot easily reach an accurate assessment of the protection available without first performing some basic research. This chapter and the ones that follow intend to equip you to better understand the liability issue.

Before beginning a discussion of liability protection provided under the rental contract, defining the following terms and concept might prove helpful:

Third-party liability claims: Bodily injury and property damage claims made by individuals (or other entities) who suffer a financial loss resulting from an accident for which the operator of the rental vehicle is legally liable.

Liability protection: When a rental company provides a renter with automobile liability protection, it agrees to pay for liability claims for which the renter or other authorized driver becomes legally liable as a result of an accident. The liability protection provided by the rental company may be primary or secondary.

Limit of liability protection: The amount of liability protection or insurance provided by the rental contract. This amount can be stated in terms of split limits or a combined single limit. Split limits (i.e., 20/40/10) are stated as bodily injury per person (the maximum that will be paid for any one bodily injury claim resulting from an accident) / bodily injury per occurrence (the maximum that will be paid for all bodily injury claims resulting from an accident) / property damage per occurrence (the maximum that will be paid for all property damage claims resulting from an accident). A combined single limit (i.e., $1 million CSL) refers to the maximum amount that will be paid for the total of all claims resulting from an accident.

Financial responsibility limit: The minimum amount of liability protection that is required by state law. This limit is sometimes also referred to as the "statutory minimum limit" or "state minimum limit."

Primary liability protection: When the rental company provides primary liability protection, its protection applies first before any other liability protection or insurance available to the renter is called upon. The limit of liability protection provided by the rental company is stated in the rental contract and is usually equal to the applicable state financial responsibility limit.

Secondary liability protection: When the rental company provides secondary liability protection, its protection applies only after all other insurance or protection available to the renter is exhausted. The rental company's secondary protection may be either "excess" or "supplemental." When it is excess, the limit stated in the rental contract is layered on top of the renter's personal insurance or protection. For example, if the renter has personal insurance limits of 20/40/10 and the rental contract provides the same limits, the renter will have a total of 40/80/20 available in the event of an accident.

When the secondary protection is supplemental, the rental company provides only the amount of liability protection required to fill the gap between the renter's personal coverage and the amount required by state law. For example, if the renter has personal insurance with limits of 20/40/10 and the state financial responsibility requirement is 30/60/20, the rental company would provide limits of protection no greater than 10/20/10 (the difference between the renter's personal coverage and the required state limit). If the state financial responsibility requirement was 20/40/10, then the rental company would provide no liability protection.

Insurance vs. self-insurance: Rental car companies protect themselves and their customers against third-party liability claims by either purchasing insurance or deciding to self-insure this exposure. Self-insurance is often used as an alternative to commercial insurance because of its potentially lower costs. Under a program of self-insurance, instead of purchasing liability coverage from an insurance company, the rental company must establish a special reserve out of which claims will be paid. A company must first obtain the approval of the state before it can operate as a self-insurer. In addition to the financial ability to pay potential claims, the state also considers the company's ability to assume or otherwise obtain services that are normally provided by an insurer.

Smaller independent rental companies and franchisees of larger companies are more likely to purchase liability insurance from an insurer. Larger rental companies are more likely to have the financial and administrative resources needed to qualify as self-insurers. But no rental company relies solely on self-insurance in treating liability exposures. Most use self-insurance for their primary "layer" of liability protection and then rely upon traditional insurance coverage for excess protection. The layer of self-insurance retained by the larger companies can extend up to million of dollars.

RENTAL CAR LIABILITY PROTECTION: A HISTORICAL PERSPECTIVE

Liability protection provided by rental companies is the source of much confusion and misunderstanding. Many customers discover that their rental contract provides little, if any, protection only after it is too late.

It wasn't always this way. Rental companies used to routinely provide renters with relatively high limits as part of the rental transaction. Renters could expect to receive liability limits of 100/300/25, which was usually adequate for most. It wasn't necessary to be too concerned about liability exposure when renting a car.

But after a period of rapidly escalating liability costs during the early 1990s, the industry took a hard look at the problem and decided to reduce the level of liability protection provided to customers to the absolute minimum required by law. They first reduced this liability protection to meet the state financial responsibility requirements. They next decided to venture into the area of "secondary" liability protection.

The thought of not providing even a minimum level of liability protection to renters was quite revolutionary. Customers had always been provided with liability protection in the past, even if at a relatively low limit. When you rented a car, you just assumed that the rental company would protect you if you had an accident. Now, the companies were telling you that you had to use your own insurance policy if you wanted protection!

The concept of making a renter's personal or business auto insurance primary generated some unfavorable publicity for the industry. Articles with titles such as "Car Rental Companies Slash Insurance Coverage" began to appear in *Consumer Reports Travel Letter* and other publications. Once again, the rental industry did a poor job of explaining and justifying its decision, so the resulting public perception was largely negative.

Had the industry done a better job of explaining the reasons behind this decision perhaps the reaction would not have been so critical. For example, the industry failed to communicate:

- The extent of its accident-related costs. The public would have been astounded at the millions of dollars spent each year in the settlement and defense of liability claims.
- That many renters already have adequate insurance available that will protect them while driving a rental car.
- That rental rates would have gone up for everyone (not just those who had accidents) if the responsibility for accident costs had not been shifted. Shifting primary liability responsibility to the renter allows the rental companies to keep their daily rates as low as possible for all, especially those who don't have accidents.

DETERMINING WHETHER YOU HAVE PRIMARY OR SECONDARY LIABILITY PROTECTION UNDER THE RENTAL CONTRACT

Understanding whether the rental company will provide you with primary or secondary liability protection is not easy. It can become a rather complex issue, contingent on a number of factors.

Unfortunately, renters often become involved in a "tug-of-war" over the coverage issue because of various objectives that are at work (and often in conflict):

- To contain its accident costs, the rental company wants to shift the liability exposure to your insurance company.
- Your insurer wants to avoid this exposure, so it wants the rental company to retain the primary liability responsibility.
- You become "stuck in the middle" and simply want someone to provide you with protection.

To determine how this conflict between the rental company and your insurance company is ultimately resolved requires the careful consideration of several factors:

The existence of applicable state law

Some states have laws in place that specifically allow for the shifting of the primary liability obligation from the owner of the vehicle (the rental company) to the renter's insurer. In those states, any other insurance you have available will be primary to that of the rental company.

In other states, laws require the rental company to provide primary liability protection. Your own insurance does not come into play until the limits provided by the rental company are exhausted.

The primary/secondary question is less clear in the remaining states. In the absence of a specific statute on the issue, the courts tend to review the issue on a case-by-case basis. Decisions are based on existing case law (judicial determination of past similar situations) and the courts' interpretation of the language contained in the rental contract and your insurance policies.

Rental contract language

Rental companies exercise great care in drafting their rental contract language, especially the provisions relating to the priority of liability protection. The companies' objective is to shift the responsibility for providing liability protection to your insurer when possible.

Rental contracts typically contain a provision stating that the rental company's protection does not apply until all other liability insurance or protection available to the renter and/or the driver of the rental vehicle is exhausted. If the renter's other liability protection is exhausted, the protection provided by the car rental company will be limited to the amount required to meet the applicable state financial responsibility requirement.

By clearly stating that its protection will not apply until other protection available to the renter is exhausted, the rental company establishes its secondary liability position.

Insurance policy language

Courts also review the language contained in your personal insurance policies to determine the priority of coverage, particularly those policy provisions relating to nonowned automobiles and "other insurance."

The "other insurance" provision of the standard ISO personal auto policy coverage form reads: "If there is other applicable liability insurance, we will pay only our share of the loss. Our share is the proportion that our limit bears to the total of all applicable limits. However, any insurance we provide for a vehicle you do not own shall be excess over any other collectible insurance."

Because the renter obviously does not own the rental car, the insurance company takes the position that the coverage provided by its policy is excess to that provided by the car rental company.

Insurance vs. self-insurance

The fact that some car rental companies purchase liability insurance and others decide to self-insure their liability exposure was previously discussed. This often impacts the primary/secondary liability protection issue.

The "other insurance" provision of a personal auto policy states that the coverage provided by that policy "shall be excess over any other collectible insurance." Rental companies often take the position that when they are self-insured, there is no other "collectible insurance" available, so the coverage provided by the personal auto policy becomes primary. When a rental company buys insurance instead of being self-insured, it usually loses this argument.

This important issue is often decided on such technicalities. The determining factor becomes how the courts interpret the language of the rental contract and insurance policies. The courts generally rule in one of the following ways:

- The rental company is responsible for providing primary liability protection.
- Your personal insurance carrier is responsible for providing primary protection.
- There should be some type of sharing of responsibility for primary liability protection between the rental company and your insurer. This sharing is typically pro rata on the basis of the proportion of aggregate liability protection available from both sources. (For example, if the rental company provided a per person liability limit of $50,000 and the limit of your personal insurance policy is $100,000, any liability claim payment would be shared with the rental company paying one-third the amount and your insurer two-thirds.)

All of this may seem confusing, but there is no way to simplify this extremely complex issue. It is often decided on a case-by-case basis and can change at a moment's notice. Rental companies are constantly updating the language in their contracts, and insurers are doing the same with their policies.

DETERMINING THE LIMIT OF LIABILITY PROTECTION PROVIDED BY THE RENTAL COMPANY

The limit or amount of liability protection provided by the rental company is also dependent on a number of factors:

When the rental company's liability protection is primary

When rental companies do provide primary liability protection, they typically provide no more than the minimum amount of protection required by the applicable state financial responsibility law.

Which state law is "applicable" is often determined by the terms of the rental contract. Some contracts state that the laws of the state where the rental contract was signed will prevail. Others state that the laws of the state where the accident occurs will apply. In some cases, a controversy arises among parties, and the question of which state's laws will apply must be decided in the courts.

When the rental company provides primary protection, your personal liability insurance will apply up to the limit of your policy after the rental company's limit is exhausted. The total limit of liability protection available to you would equal the sum of the limit provided by your rental contract and the limit of your personal insurance policy.

81

When the rental company's liability protection is secondary

When the liability protection provided by the rental company is secondary, all other protection available to you from any source applies first. If the limit of protection provided by your policies is exhausted, the rental company may or may not provide you with any additional protection.

The rental contract used by some rental companies states that their liability protection will be in excess over other available liability protection. This means that the full limit of protection provided under the terms of the rental contract (usually the applicable state financial responsibility limit) will apply after your other coverage is exhausted. So your total liability protection would again be the sum of the limits of your personal insurance and the limit afforded by the rental contract.

Most rental companies use language in their contracts that states that their liability protection will supplement your other protection only to the extent needed to meet the applicable state financial responsibility requirement. This type of protection is referred to as supplemental or "gap" insurance.

In most cases, this "gap" liability protection provided by the rental company will rarely come into play when you have other coverage available. It provides absolutely no protection once the state financial responsibility requirement is met. Because most personal auto policies will increase your liability limits when required to comply with state law, it is unlikely that the rental company's protection would ever trigger. The effect is that the rental company usually provides no protection when you have any other personal or business auto coverage available to you.

When you have no other insurance available to you

What happens when the rental company provides secondary liability protection but you don't have any other insurance available to you? Are you simply left without any liability protection?

One of the primary objectives of our legal system is to ensure that innocent accident victims are adequately compensated for their injuries or damage. As a general rule, courts don't really care who pays the claims as long as the victims are compensated.

To free the rental company of financial obligation when the renter has no other coverage would violate this principle. The accident victim would remain uncompensated. For that reason, the courts tend to require rental companies to assume the primary liability responsibility when no other insurance is available. The rental company shifts from a secondary to a primary liability position when a renter is otherwise uninsured.

Uninsured/underinsured motorist coverage

Most rental contracts state that the protection provided by the rental company does not include uninsured motorist or underinsured motorist coverage, personal injury protection, no-fault insurance, or any other first-party protection that can be waived or rejected.

When individual state laws mandate such coverage, the limits provided by the rental company generally will not exceed the minimum limit required by law. If the rental company is required by law to provide any of these coverages, it will provide the lowest amount of coverage possible.

Family member exclusion

The rental contract sometimes excludes bodily injury liability claims made by family members who reside with the renter or driver of the rental vehicle. This exclusion is dependant on whether such a provision is allowed by applicable state law.

Effect of contract violations

If you violate one of the use restrictions listed in the rental contract, the company may void any liability protection that would have otherwise been provided to you in the absence of the violation.

Depending on the individual circumstances and applicable state law, this could affect you in several ways. In some states, rental companies are allowed to deny liability protection as a result of certain contract violations, thus shifting the primary liability responsibility to your insurance carrier. If you have no other liability insurance, the rental company may still be required to provide the state minimum limit but could have a right of indemnification against you.

Indemnification of the rental company

Most rental contracts contain a broad indemnification provision by which you agree to indemnify the rental company when it incurs liability costs and:

- You are not entitled to that protection under the terms of the contract.
- You would otherwise be entitled to that protection but are in violation of a use restriction.
- You are in violation of any provision of the rental contract that results in the rental company incurring costs.

Any indemnification sought by the rental company from a renter is subject to whether such recovery is allowed under applicable state law.

VICARIOUS LIABILITY OF THE RENTAL COMPANY

The laws pertaining to rental cars are influenced in a number of states by what are commonly referred to as vicarious liability statutes. Although this liability imposed on car rental companies does not directly affect the liability protection provided to a renter, there is an indirect relationship.

Vicarious liability laws are an outgrowth of the concept of "dangerous instrumentalities." Years ago, laws were written to place a higher standard of care on individuals who gave "dangerous objects" to others to use. In order make sure the owner of the instrumentality used great care in deciding who to allow to use the object, the laws held the owner vicariously liable for the acts of the borrower.

Vicarious liability laws as they apply to rental cars follow this principle. Some states consider motor vehicles to be dangerous instrumentalities and impose the same high standards on vehicle owners. Vicarious liability laws assume that the party owning the vehicle obviously has some assets, so it is better to make the owner financially responsible to injured parties than the driver, who might not have any means to compensate victims.

The result is an extremely high standard placed on car rental companies. In states governed by vicarious liability laws, the rental company becomes vicariously liable for the acts of the driver. The degree of care exercised by the rental company is not relevant. Once the company gives a car to a customer, it becomes responsible.

There have been cases in which renters caused accidents through gross negligence (such as driving under the influence or reckless driving) and the rental company was still held responsible. In this respect, these laws seem to miss the mark. They were intended to ensure that the rental company used care in renting its vehicles, but the effect seems to free renters from the responsibility to operate the vehicles safely and responsibly.

There are only a handful of states that still have vicarious liability laws. Some of them cap the amount to which a car rental company can be held financially responsible. Other states impose unlimited vicarious liability on the rental company.

Although vicarious liability laws impact the rental companies more than their customers, renters could be affected. If you have an accident and the rental company is forced to pay a large claim based on its vicarious liability, it might attempt to recover the amount from you pursuant to the indemnification provision of the rental contract.

FLUIDITY OF APPLICABLE LAW

Much of what has been discussed in this section has been qualified with the phrase "subject to applicable law" because state laws applying to rental car insurance–related issues are constantly evolving.

The issue of liability protection provided by the rental company as part of the rental transaction has been in a state of flux since the early 1990s. What used to be a relatively simple topic (the rental company provided liability protection when you rented a car) has become extremely complex. Nuances such as primary/secondary protection, liability limits, and insurance/self-insurance have caused much confusion for all involved.

When the rental industry began its attempts to shift primary liability responsibility to the renter, the insurance carriers providing renters with personal and business auto insurance reacted as expected—they resisted the effort.

Since that time, the courts have been filled with cases seeking resolution to the question of primacy. New statutes are continuously being passed and case law established on this topic. The result is an ever-changing environment in which the manner in which rental car insurance issues are handled today may be different tomorrow.

chapter eight

Protection Provided by Your Personal Auto Policy

Your personal auto policy may serve as a source of protection when renting a car. The same policy that protects you while operating your personal auto may, in certain situations, provide similar coverage when you rent.

Your personal auto policy can provide protection for both primary car rental exposures: your responsibility for vehicle damage and your legal liability to others. This chapter will discuss those exposures and the degree to which your personal auto policy provides protection for each. Also included will be some discussion of other protection that may be available under your policy when you rent, such as medical payments and uninsured motorist coverage.

We previously discussed that rental contracts contain a provision making you financially responsible for damage to the rental car. Where allowed by law, they also contain language making your other liability insurance primary while operating the rental car. This means that should you have an accident with your rental vehicle, you may need to look to your personal auto insurance carrier for needed protection.

For that reason, you should always report a rental car accident to your own insurance company just as you would if it had involved your own car. You don't want to later find out that your personal insurer might refuse to provide coverage because you failed to report the loss on a timely basis.

How do you know whether your policy will cover you in a car rental situation? The answer is not always clear and often depends on the applicable state law, the language used in the rental contract, and the language of your personal insurance policy.

Although the following discussion is intended to provide a general overview of the coverage available under a "standard" personal auto policy, any attempt to perform a precise coverage analysis is extremely difficult because of the differences that exist in the policy forms used by insurers.

This discussion will mainly focus on the current personal auto policy (PAP) form copyrighted by Insurance Services Office, Inc. (ISO), but be aware that there are numerous policy form variations currently in use. Some states do not use ISO forms, and others require modification of the ISO form by specific endorsement. Some insurers have drafted their own policy forms, and others have decided to modify the ISO form.

Therefore, you should not rely totally on this analysis without comparing this information with the language contained in your own PAP. If your policy language is different than that cited here and you are unsure of the effect, you should contact your agent with any questions you might have.

Among the various PAP forms in use, the most notable difference is the manner in which damage to the rental car is handled. Coverage for such vehicle damage may be found in either the liability or physical damage sections of the PAP, depending on which version of the policy is used.

In analyzing the ISO PAP form to determine applicability to rental situations, we will focus on the most widely used versions of the PAP. Only when there are significant differences will other PAP versions be mentioned.

Personal auto policy
The PAP is comprised of the following "coverage parts":
- Part A: Liability coverage
- Part B: Medical payments coverage
- Part C: Uninsured motorist coverage
- Part D: Coverage for damage to your auto
- Part E: Duties after an accident or loss

• Part F: General provisions

A review of each of these coverage parts in terms of its applicability to rental car situations follows.

PART A: LIABILITY COVERAGE

To analyze the extent to which part A provides liability coverage in situations involving rental cars, it is necessary to review relevant provisions contained in the insuring agreement, exclusions, and other general conditions.

Paragraph A of the insuring agreement of part A states, in part:

"We will agree to pay damages for 'bodily injury' or 'property damage' for which any 'insured' becomes legally responsible because of an auto accident."

To better understand the full intent of the insuring agreement, the term "insured" needs to be defined.

Paragraph B of the insuring agreement reads:

"'Insured' as used in this part means: you or any 'family member' for the ownership, maintenance, or use of any auto or 'trailer.'"

The policy further defines "you" as the policyholder and spouse, if a resident of the same household.

The definitions section of the policy defines "family member" as:

"... a person related to you by blood, marriage, or adoption who is a resident of your household. This includes a ward or foster child."

When all of these provisions are combined, the result is that the PAP will provide liability coverage for those individuals defined as "insureds" who become legally responsible for bodily injury or property damage resulting from an auto accident and arising out of the ownership, maintenance, or use of any auto. Because the definition of "any auto" would include a nonowned rental car, liability coverage would be available in rental situations.

Of course, this extension of liability coverage to rental vehicles is subject to all of the relevant exclusions and limitations included in the policy. But the important point is that liability coverage is available under this policy form for the car rental exposure under certain circumstances.

Other insurance

What if your rental car accident could be covered under more than one policy? In that case, the other insurance provision of the PAP will come into play.

This provision states:

"If there is other applicable insurance, we will pay only our share of the loss. Our share is the proportion that our limit of liability bears to the total of all applicable limits. However, any insurance we provide for a vehicle you do not own shall be excess over any other collectible insurance."

This other insurance provision often conflicts with language contained in the rental contract. In states where a rental company is permitted to adopt a secondary liability position, the rental contract says that any other liability protection available to the renter will be primary. The PAP says that any other insurance (including that covering the rental car) shall be primary. In the absence of statute or controlling case law, this conflict is often resolved by sharing liability payments on a pro rata basis.

When attempting to resolve an other insurance issue, you must always consider the actual language of the personal auto policy, the rental contract, and any applicable statutes and/or case law. Some states have laws or regulations that specify the primacy of coverage between that of the renter and the rental company. In other states, the controlling factor is established case law. In either situation, the primacy issue is dynamic and can change at any time with the next court decision or legislative act.

Limits of liability

The limits of liability listed in the policy declarations of the PAP will apply to rental car situations. Your policy provides the same limits when a nonowned vehicle such as a rental car is involved as when you are using your own car.

Damage to the rental car

The liability coverage provided in part A of the current PAP form used in most states does not include coverage for damage to the rental vehicle.

Exclusion A3 of the policy states:

"We do not provide liability coverage for any 'insured': for 'property damage' to property: rented to, used by, or in the care of that 'insured.'"

If your rental vehicle is damaged, part A of your PAP will not provide liability coverage for that damage because of this exclusion. Any damage to the rental car for which you are responsible is instead handled under your policy's physical damage coverage in part D.

There is an exception, however. The PAP form used in a few states (Minnesota, New York, North Carolina, North Dakota, Rhode Island, and

Texas) does provide coverage for damage to your rental car under part A liability coverage. This is accomplished by adding either an exception to the above-mentioned exclusion or a specific rental car coverage endorsement.

To illustrate, the care, custody, and control exclusion in Minnesota is amended to include the following language:

"This exclusion does not apply to: b. Liability assumed under contract for property damage to a rented: private passenger auto, pickup or van, truck with a registered gross vehicle weight of 26,000 pounds or less if the rate for use of the rented vehicle is determined on a daily or weekly basis."

The effect of this provision is to eliminate the exclusion and include coverage for damage to the rental car under the liability coverage section of the PAP.

Does it make any difference to you whether your PAP handles damage to the rental car under its liability coverage section or coverage for damage to your auto section?

It is often to your advantage if your policy covers the damage under its liability coverage section instead of the coverage for damage to your auto section because:

- For damage to be covered under the policy's part D coverage for damage to your auto section, your policy must include physical damage coverage for the vehicles you own. If your personal auto does not include collision coverage, you will not have collision coverage for the rental car either. If your policy includes liability coverage, the damage to the rental car would be covered regardless of whether it also included collision coverage.

- When handled under part D, damage to the rental car will be subject to the deductible that appears on your policy, and you will be responsible for that deductible amount. In contrast, liability coverage does not include a deductible.

- Part D may not include coverage for "indirect damages" such as loss of use or administrative fees. Under the liability coverage section of the PAP, all costs for which you are legally liable to the rental company would be covered.

On the other hand, there is one advantage in having the damage to the rental car covered under the part D coverage for damage to your auto section. When handled under the liability coverage section, the damage to the rental car is subject to the liability limits of your policy. If you carry minimum limits on your policy, those limits may not be adequate. For example, your property damage limit may be as low as $10,000. With the current value of automobiles, the damage to the rental car could easily exceed that limit.

PART B: MEDICAL PAYMENTS COVERAGE

The standard PAP also includes coverage for medical expenses incurred by an insured under its part B medical payments coverage. The following discussion of part B addresses the availability of medical payments coverage in a rental situation.

Paragraph A of the part B insuring agreement states:

"We will pay reasonable expenses incurred for necessary medical and funeral services because of 'bodily injury': (1) caused by an accident and (2) sustained by an 'insured.'"

Paragraph B goes on to define "insured" by stating:

"'Insured' as used in this Part means: you or any 'family member' ... while 'occupying' ... a motor vehicle designed for use mainly on public roads."

Because there is no requirement that the vehicle must be an owned vehicle, the result is that the policy does extend medical payments coverage to the policyholder and "family members" (same definition as in part A liability coverage) when occupying a nonowned vehicle, including a rental car.

But once again, this part is subject to the other insurance provision, which states:

"If there is other applicable auto medical payments insurance, we will pay only our share of the loss. Our share is the proportion that our limit of liability bears to the total of all applicable limits. However, any insurance we provide with respect to a vehicle you do not own shall be excess over any other collectible auto insurance providing payments for medical or funeral expenses."

The rental contract used by most rental companies contains language stating that medical payments coverage will not be provided unless required by law. As a result, coverage is usually available only under the PAP, and this other insurance provision rarely applies.

PART C: UNINSURED MOTORIST COVERAGE

The applicability of part C uninsured motorist coverage of the PAP is relatively consistent with that of part B. Paragraph A of its insuring agreement reads:

"We will pay compensatory damages which an 'insured' is legally entitled to recover from the owner or operator of an 'uninsured motor vehicle' because of 'bodily injury': (1) sustained by an 'insured' and (2) caused by an accident."

Paragraph B of the part C insuring agreement further states:

"'Insured' as used in this part means: (1) you or any 'family member.'"

Part C also contains an other insurance provision that states:

"If there is other applicable insurance available under one or more policies or provisions of coverage: (2) Any insurance we provide with respect to a vehicle you do not own shall be excess over any collectible insurance providing coverage on a primary basis."

Again, rental contracts generally state that uninsured motorist coverage will not be included unless the rental company is required by law to provide such coverage. When applicable law does require UM coverage to be included in the rental transaction, it is usually provided on a primary basis with limits up to the state minimum financial responsibility limit.

PART D: COVERAGE FOR DAMAGE TO YOUR AUTO

That there is usually no coverage available for such damage under the liability coverage section of the PAP was previously discussed. The following analysis describes the extent to which coverage for damage to the rented vehicle may be provided under part D coverage for damage to your auto.

Paragraph A of the part D insuring agreement states:

"We will pay for direct and accidental loss to 'your covered auto' or any 'nonowned auto,' including their equipment, minus any applicable deductible shown in the declarations."

In analyzing the coverage available in a rental situation under part D, it is necessary to define the terms "your covered auto" and "nonowned auto." The definitions section of the policy says that "your covered auto" means:

"(1) Any vehicle shown in the declarations, (2) Any ... vehicles on the date you become the owner (provided) you acquire the vehicle during the policy period (and) ... ask us to insure it within 30 days after you become the owner."

Clearly, the definition of "your covered auto" is intended to include only those vehicles you own or acquire during the policy term and not rental vehicles. So it becomes necessary to next look at the definition of "nonowned auto."

The definition of "nonowned auto" is not found in the PAP definitions section but instead in the insuring agreement of part D because the definition has applicability only to part D. In paragraph C of the part D insuring agreement, "nonowned auto" is defined as:

"(1) Any private passenger auto, pickup, van, or 'trailer' not owned by or furnished or available for the regular use of you or any 'family member while in the custody of or being operated by you or any family member' or (2) any auto or 'trailer' you do not own while used as a temporary substitute for 'your covered auto,' which is out of normal use because of its: (a) breakdown, (b) repair, (c) servicing, (d) loss, or (e) destruction."

The first definition would apply to a rental situation and would provide for physical damage coverage under part D. The phrase "furnished or available for the regular use" is not defined in the PAP, but it has been tested in the courts and has been generally established not to include short-term rentals.

The current prevailing position of insurance companies is not to consider a short-term rental to fall within this "furnished or available for regular use" limitation. Of course, the longer the rental period, the more likely the PAP insurer might consider the "furnished or available for regular use" limitation to apply. The coverage determination then becomes dependent upon the specific situation and the insurer's interpretation of this provision.

The second definition could also apply to a rental vehicle but only when the rental was replacing your covered auto while your auto was out of service as a result of breakdown, repair, servicing, loss, or destruction. The overall effect is that the part D insuring agreement clearly extends physical damage coverage to a rental vehicle, subject to other policy conditions.

But as with the policy's liability coverage, the extension of physical damage coverage under the PAP is not without limitations. The definition of "nonowned auto" is limited to vehicles "while in the custody of or being operated by you or any family member." Is there coverage under the PAP if you rent a car and allow a friend to drive it?

Probably not because the vehicle was not in the possession of you or a family member when damaged. The primary responsibility would probably fall upon the PAP insurer of the friend who did have possession of the vehicle. If your friend had no insurance and your policy didn't provide coverage, you could find yourself personally responsible for the damage on the basis of your contractual responsibility.

Coverage for physical damage to your owned vehicle is provided for vehicles listed on your policy declarations. For each vehicle listed on the policy, the declarations also show the type of physical damage coverage (collision and/or other than collision) and the deductible amount that applies. But what type of coverage and deductible applies to a "nonowned auto" such as a rental car?

The answer is found in paragraph A of the part D insuring agreement, which states:

"If there is a loss to a 'nonowned auto,' we will provide the broadest coverage applicable to any 'your covered auto' shown in the declarations."

To illustrate, assume that you have three vehicles scheduled on your PAP. One has collision coverage and other than collision (sometimes referred to as "comprehensive") coverage, both with a $100 deductible. The second vehicle has collision and other than collision coverage, both with a $500 deductible. The third has liability but no physical damage coverage.

You have an accident in a rental car that results in damage to the vehicle. Your PAP would provide you with collision coverage with a $100 deductible, which is the "broadest coverage applicable to any vehicle defined as 'your covered auto' and scheduled in the declarations."

A good way to define the term "broadest coverage applicable" is to determine which vehicle's coverage would be of greatest benefit to you as policyholder. The intent of your insurer is to provide the most favorable coverage available under your policy.

Whenever you rent a car, you should keep this "broadest coverage available" concept in mind. If your PAP provides physical damage coverage for any of the cars listed on your policy, you will have coverage for damage to the rental vehicle. The deductible that will be applied by your insurance company will be the most favorable (i.e., lowest) to you.

Some policies contain an exception to the "broadest coverage" rule when your rental car serves as a "temporary substitute vehicle" by replacing your personal auto while it is out of service or being repaired. Under some policies, when the rental is considered a temporary substitute, the coverage provided will be the same as for the vehicle on your policy that is out of service.

What is the limit of liability provided under part D of your PAP in a rental situation? The limit of liability section of part D states:

"Our limit of liability for loss will be the lesser of the: (1) actual cash value of the stolen or damaged property; (2) amount necessary to repair or replace the property with other property of like kind and quality."

The fact that there is no distinction between "your covered auto" and a "nonowned auto" is very significant. Say that you own a vehicle having an actual cash value of $10,000 and insure it under your PAP. You rent a car worth $30,000, and it is "totaled" in an accident. Even though you paid a premium commensurate with a $10,000 vehicle, your policy will provide coverage up to the full $30,000 actual cash value of the rental car.

Although it is less common, some policy forms include provisions limiting the maximum amount payable under your PAP coverage to the value of the vehicle listed on your policy. Under this type of provision, if your personal vehicle is worth $10,000, that would be the maximum the policy would pay for damage to the rental car. If so, you could find this limitation insufficient to cover the value of the rental car.

If you damage the rental car and the rental company seeks an additional amount under a loss of turn-back value claim, your PAP would probably not cover that additional amount. You could be left personally responsible for the difference.

Whenever rental car damage is covered under your policy's physical damage coverage, you will be responsible for the deductible amount listed on your policy. If you have a high deductible, it might be wise to consider the purchase of the rental company's loss damage waiver (LDW).

The terms of the rental contract also hold you responsible for the company's loss of use and administrative charges resulting from damage to the rental vehicle. Does the PAP also cover those items of indirect damage?

Under part D, the section titled "Transportation Expenses" states:

"In addition, we will pay, without application of a deductible, up to $15 per day, to a maximum of $450 for: loss of use expenses for which you become legally responsible in the event of loss to a 'nonowned auto.' Our payment will be limited to that period of time reasonably required to repair or replace ... the 'nonowned auto.'"

Although this provision does provide coverage for any loss of use claimed by the rental company, there are limitations on both the allowed period of time and the maximum amount per day. This limit may be insufficient if the rental company calculates its loss of use on the basis of the daily rental rate, which could be as high as $40 or $50 per day. If the daily limit in the PAP for transportation expenses is less, you could still be left financially responsible for the balance of the rental company's claim.

In order for coverage for transportation expenses under part D to apply, you must have the appropriate coverage on your PAP. If the rental company's loss of use claim is the result of you being involved in a collision, your PAP must include collision coverage for the transportation expense coverage to apply. If the loss was the result of a windstorm, your PAP must include other than collision coverage.

Finally, there is also no provision in the PAP that provides for payment of any administrative fee billed by the rental company. If the rental company pursues payment of its administrative fee, it will likely remain your personal responsibility.

Part D of the PAP also contains several significant exclusions. The exclusions section of the policy states:

"We will not pay for: (4) loss to: (a) any electronic equipment designed for the reproduction of sound; (b) any other electronic equipment that receives or transmits audio, visual, or data signals."

The policy further states that this exclusion does not apply to (1) sound reproducing equipment that is permanently installed in the vehicle, removable from a housing unit that is permanently installed, and designed to be powered by the vehicle's electrical system or (2) any other electronic equipment that is necessary for the normal operation of the vehicle or the monitoring of the vehicle's operating system.

What does this mean to you in a rental situation? One possible implication is that there may be no coverage for portable telephones or the electronic navigation devices that are sometimes installed in rental vehicles.

Another policy exclusion eliminates coverage for:

"Loss to or loss of use of a 'nonowned auto' rented by: (a) you or (b) any 'family member' if a rental vehicle company is precluded from recovering such loss or loss of use from you or that family member pursuant to the provisions of any applicable rental agreement or state law."

This exclusion applies when (1) the rental occurs in a state that has a law limiting the renter's financial responsibility for vehicle damage or when (2) you purchase the LDW. This provision prevents the rental company from seeking payment from your PAP insurer when it has no legal basis to recover the damages directly from you, as renter of the vehicle.

PART E: DUTIES AFTER AN ACCIDENT OR LOSS

Your PAP requires you to notify your insurance company on a timely basis when an accident occurs. Part E of the PAP states:

"We have no duty to provide coverage under this policy unless there has been full compliance with the following duties: We must be notified promptly of how, when, and where the accident or loss happened. Notice should also include the names of any injured persons and of any witnesses."

You have a dual reporting duty if you have an accident with a rental car. The terms of your rental contract require you to immediately report the accident to the rental company. But because most rental contracts state that any insurance available to you will apply first, you also need to report the matter to your personal auto insurance company or any other insurance company that may provide coverage for the loss.

Your obligation does not end when you report the accident to the rental company. The rental company will not report it to your personal auto insurance company for you. That is your responsibility, and failing to do so could jeopardize the coverage available under your policy.

PART F: GENERAL PROVISIONS

The PAP includes several general provisions that could become relevant if you have an accident with a rental car.

Coverage territory

The PAP provides coverage within the United States (including its territories and possessions), Puerto Rico, and Canada. When you rent a vehicle outside of this coverage territory, do not expect your PAP to respond.

Limitation on rental coverage

Although not contained in the standard PAP, some insurers include policy provisions limiting coverage in car rental situations. The most common limitations include the following:

- The length of the rental period (i.e., no more than 21 consecutive days)
- The aggregate number of annual rental days (i.e., no more than 45 of the preceding 365 days)
- The purpose of the rental (i.e., no coverage for business use)

Insurance policies that limit coverage for rental car situations sometimes offer to sell that coverage back to you in the form of a policy endorsement. For an additional premium, the insurance company may remove these limitations and even include additional coverage for items, such as the car rental company's administrative fee, that would not ordinarily be covered under your policy.

Prior to renting, you should be aware of any such limitations that might be included in your policy. If your policy contains any limitations, you should ask your agent whether expanded coverage is available and whether you need it.

Right to recover payment

The PAP includes a provision that states that if a payment is made under the policy, your insurance company has the right to seek recovery of that payment from other parties who may be legally responsible for the damages. You, as the PAP policyholder, are required to do whatever possible to assist the insurer and not jeopardize your insurer's rights.

Accident claims involving rental cars can become quite confusing with the number of entities involved and questions about the priority of coverage. It is entirely possible that your PAP insurer, the rental company, your credit card company, and the insurance carriers of other involved parties might all be actively involved in the process.

It is therefore important that you do not sign any releases of other documents without having your insurance company first review them. You don't want to violate this provision of your PAP by releasing any responsible parties, thus prejudicing the rights of your insurer.

WHAT TO ASK YOUR INSURANCE AGENT

Because of the many different variations of PAP forms in the marketplace, it is impossible to advise you with certainty whether yours will provide coverage when you are involved in an accident with a rental car. Therefore, it is recommended that you seek the advice of your insurance agent prior to renting.

When doing so, make sure you clearly explain the particulars of your intended rental. Inform the agent where you will be renting, for how long, the type of vehicle you've reserved, the reason you're renting a car, and who will be driving. Only with complete information can your agent determine whether your policy will cover you.

Some of the specific information you might want to provide and questions you might want to ask your agent include:

- Why you are renting a car (i.e., vacation, business trip, personal car is in the shop for repairs, etc.). Will your policy cover you while operating the rental vehicle under those circumstances?
- The type of vehicle you're planning to rent. Will your policy provide coverage for that vehicle? Some policies exclude coverage for expensive, exotic, or antique cars, so if you are planning to rent a Lamborghini, you need to ask whether it will be covered.

- Will your policy handle damage to the rental car under its liability coverage or its physical damage (collision and other than collision) coverage?
- If the damage will be covered under your policy's liability coverage, are your property damage limits sufficient to pay for the full value of the rental car in the event a total loss occurs?
- If damage is covered under your physical damage coverage, is the amount of your coverage limited to the value of the vehicle(s) on your policy, or will it cover the entire value of the rental car if its value is higher than the one you own?
- Will your policy cover loss of use and administrative charges billed by the rental company?
- Will you be responsible for a deductible? How much?
- Will the insurance company increase your premium or possibly cancel your policy if you make a claim under your personal auto policy?

Only after you fully understand the answers to these questions can you accurately assess your potential financial exposure and decide whether your own coverage is adequate or whether you should consider the purchase any of the optional protection from the rental company.

chapter nine

Protection Provided by Your Business Auto Policy

The preceding chapter described the coverage that may be available under your personal auto policy when renting a car. But what if you are renting for business purposes?

Rather than a personal auto policy, the appropriate place to find coverage in most business rental situations is under a commercial auto coverage form (referred to hereafter as a business auto policy, or BAP). Most companies with any type of automobile exposure generally choose to insure that risk under some form of BAP.

There are variations in today's marketplace, but this discussion will focus on the business auto coverage form CA 00 01 (7/97) filed by the Insurance Services Office, Inc.

Companies owning automobiles used for business purposes are well aware of the need to insure that exposure. But companies without owned vehicles still have an auto exposure resulting from the use of nonowned vehicles such as rental cars in business activities.

In determining whether a BAP provides coverage in a car rental situation, the first step is to address the manner in which the BAP form describes covered autos by examining the covered auto designation symbols listed on the policy declaration page.

A PAP requires that you specifically list the auto(s) you own on your policy. But businesses sometimes need to have flexibility in their designation of covered autos, especially if they change vehicles with some frequency or use nonowned vehicles. This flexibility is achieved through the use of covered auto symbols that allow you to select the classification of covered autos and coverage most appropriate for your particular auto exposure.

The symbols used with the ISO policy form include:

1. Any "auto": This is the broadest covered auto definition provided. It includes any auto whether owned, borrowed, rented, or used by the named insured as indicated on the policy. When coverage symbol 1 is used, there is no need to also select any other symbol because symbol 1 provides the broadest possible coverage.

Symbol 1 is used for liability coverage only. Having this symbol on the policy ensures that the named insured does have coverage for rental cars used for business purposes.

2. Owned "autos" only: Coverage is provided only for vehicles that are owned by the named insured or acquired during the policy period. This symbol provides no coverage for nonowned vehicles including rental cars.

3. Owned private passenger "autos" only: This symbol is comparable to symbol 2, except it provides coverage for owned passenger vehicles only, whereas symbol 2 also extends coverage for trailers or semi-trailers. Symbol 3 provides no coverage for rented cars.

4. Owned "autos" other than private passenger "autos" only: In contrast to symbol 3, symbol 4 provides coverage only for owned vehicles other than passenger vehicles. But like symbol 2 and symbol 3, there is no coverage for rented vehicles.

5. Owned "autos" subject to no-fault: This symbol is used when autos you own are required by applicable state law to have no-fault insurance coverage. Symbol 5 does not apply to nonowned vehicles including rental cars.

6. Owned "autos" subject to a compulsory uninsured motorist law: Symbol 6 is similar to symbol 5, except it applies to uninsured motorist rather than no-fault coverage. Again, this symbol does not apply to rental cars.

7. Specifically described "autos": Symbol 7 is probably the most narrowly defined classification. It requires vehicles to be specifically scheduled on the policy for coverage to apply. This requirement makes the use of this symbol inappropriate for nonowned vehicles, so it should not be considered in protecting against the car rental exposure.

8. Hired "autos" only: Symbol 8 provides coverage for vehicles leased, hired, rented, or borrowed by the named insured. It does not include vehicles leased, hired, rented, or borrowed from any of the named insured's employees, partners, or members of their households. This symbol does provide coverage for rental vehicles when rented by the named insured.

9. Nonowned "autos" only: Symbol 9 covers vehicles that the named insured does not own, lease, hire, rent, or borrow used in connection with the named insured's business. Included are vehicles owned by the named insured's employees, partners, and members of their households. There is no coverage for vehicles rented by the named insured. Symbol 9 is used for liability coverage only.

LIABILITY COVERAGE UNDER THE BAP

On the basis of this brief overview, liability coverage may be available for rental cars by using symbols 1, 8, and/or 9. However, there are some significant differences in the manner in which rental cars are handled under each of these three symbols.

Before describing the implications of using each of these symbols, the definitions of the terms "named insured" and "insured" should be clarified. The term "named insured" refers to the individual or business entity listed on the BAP declarations page on the line titled "named insured." Throughout the BAP form, any reference to "you" or "your" refers specifically to the named insured.

The BAP also uses the term "insured." For example, the liability coverage insuring agreement states, "We will pay all sums an 'insured' legally must pay as damages because of bodily injury or property damage to which this insurance applies, caused by an accident and resulting from the ownership, maintenance, or use of a covered auto."

Under the BAP, there are three categories of "insureds." The first is the aforementioned named insured. The second is the permissive user of a covered auto or an individual using a vehicle defined as a covered auto with the permission of the named insured. The third category refers to anyone liable for the conduct of an insured. This might include a supervisor or manager of a permissive user who is not the named insured. The intent is to provide liability protection through the entire chain of authority in a permissive user situation.

There are several exceptions to the second and third categories of insured, but they are not relevant to this discussion. The important point is that there is a distinction between the terms "named insured" and "insured" that affects the application of coverage under the BAP.

SYMBOL 1: ANY AUTO

Using symbol 1 provides coverage for virtually any vehicle used in connection with the named insured's business. It provides the broadest protection and is most beneficial from the policyholder's perspective. However, the broad protection is not without cost because the premium charged by the insurer will be commensurate with the increased exposure.

But even if you decide that the premium is well worth the peace of mind that comes with the broadest coverage, you may have difficulty finding a carrier willing to offer it. Insurers typically do not make it available for physical damage coverage and may even be reluctant to provide it for liability protection unless they feel comfortable with the nature of the exposure. So before quickly deciding to select symbol 1 for your BAP, you need to determine its availability and cost.

SYMBOL 8: HIRED AUTOS ONLY

Symbol 8 provides coverage for vehicles leased, hired, rented, or borrowed by the named insured. When the vehicle is leased, hired, rented, or borrowed by the named insured, coverage applies (subject to any applicable policy exclusions) when the vehicle is used by any insured, including employees of the named insured. An important distinction is that an employee who rents a car in his or her own name (and not under the name of the named insured) is not covered when symbol 8 is selected. The vehicle *must be rented in the name of the named insured.* Even when a rented vehicle is being used solely in connection with the named insured's business, there will be no coverage under symbol 8 unless the vehicle is rented under the name of the named insured.

When symbol 8 is used, it is important to instruct all employees to rent cars in the name of the named insured (presumably the business name). This symbol *requires* that the rental transaction be in the name of the policy's named insured only.

When symbol 8 is selected and a car is rented by the named insured, liability protection will be provided under the BAP. Liability coverage will also be extended to any employee of the named insured using the rental vehicle provided that he or she has the permission of the named insured. The employee qualifies as an insured by being a permissive user of the vehicle rented by the named insured.

SYMBOL 9: NONOWNED AUTOS ONLY

The selection of symbol 9 provides liability coverage for vehicles used in connection with the named insured's business when they are not owned, leased, hired, rented, or borrowed by the named insured. This might be described as the "flip side" of the situation described above involving the use of symbol 8. Symbol 9 will provide coverage to the named insured for rental vehicles used in connection with the named insured's business but only if they are not rented by the named insured. Under symbol 9, no coverage will exist if the rental transaction is made in the name of the named insured. Coverage will exist if the rental is made in an employee's name and the rental vehicle is used in connection with the named insured's business.

Be aware that a coverage gap may exist when selecting symbol 9. When an employee of the named insured rents a car in his or her own name and a loss occurs while that employee is within the scope of employment, liability coverage will be afforded to the named insured *but not necessarily to the employee.* This is because the BAP defines an insured (i.e., permissive user) as one using (with the named insured's permission) a covered auto that the named insured owns, hires, or borrows. Because the employee, rather than the named insured, has rented the car, the employee is not considered an insured under the BAP.

An employer can solve this coverage gap by adding an "employees as insureds" endorsement to the BAP. This endorsement qualifies any employee of the named insured as an insured while using a covered auto in the business of the named insured.

An "employee hired autos" endorsement may also accomplish the same purpose. This endorsement states that an employee operating a vehicle rented under his or her own name and with the permission of the named insured will be considered an insured while performing duties related to the named insured's business.

OTHER INSURANCE

The other insurance provision of the BAP states, "For any covered auto you don't own, the insurance provided by this coverage form is excess over any other collectible insurance." At first, this seems to indicate that liability coverage is provided only on an excess basis for rental cars (as nonowned autos). However, the other insurance provision goes on to state that regardless of the condition described above, "this coverage form's liability coverage is primary for any liability assumed under an 'insured contract.'"

The definitions section of the BAP defines "insured contract" as "that part of any contract or agreement entered into, as part of your business, pertaining to the rental or lease by you, or any of your employees, of any auto." By executing the rental agreement, you are, in effect, entering into an insured contract as defined by the BAP. In the event of a covered loss, the BAP should respond by providing primary liability protection.

COVERAGE TERRITORY

The coverage territory as defined in the BAP includes the United States and its possessions and territories, Puerto Rico and Canada. If you plan to rent a car outside of this territory, your BAP would not likely respond.

However, this territory limitation can be expanded to include worldwide coverage for rented cars by endorsement or use of a more recent policy form. For worldwide coverage to apply, the rental can be for no longer than 30 days and cannot include a hired driver. Also, damages must be awarded in the United States and its territories or possessions, Puerto Rico or Canada, or by settlement to which the BAP insurance company agrees.

PHYSICAL DAMAGE COVERAGE UNDER THE BAP

The above information described how to obtain liability protection under the BAP for your car rental exposure, but what about your exposure for loss of or damage to the rental vehicle?

At first glance, it may seem that your exposure for damage might fall under the liability provisions of your BAP. After all, you executed a rental contract stating that you would be responsible for all such damage. It seems to make sense that this exposure would be covered under your BAP liability coverage. However, the BAP contains a care, custody, or control exclusion that precludes any coverage under the policy's liability section.

The exclusion states that "This insurance does not apply to ... property damage to or covered pollution cost or expense involving property owned or transported by the insured or in the insured's care, custody, or control."

Finding liability coverage under the insured contract provision of the BAP described above would also seem to be a possibility. By executing the rental contract, you have contractually agreed to be responsible for any loss of or damage to the rental vehicle.

The insured contract definition goes on to state "However, such contract or agreement shall not be considered an insured contract to the extent that it obligates you or any of your employees to pay for property damage to any auto rented or leased by you or any of your employees."

On the basis of this analysis, it is clear that the only way to obtain coverage for damage to the rental vehicle is through the BAP physical damage coverage.

To ensure that coverage for damage to the rental vehicle will be available under your BAP, you must repeat the process described above by selecting the proper symbol(s) to designate what will be considered a covered auto under the policy's physical damage coverage.

The selection of symbol 1 (any auto), symbol 8 (hired autos), or symbol 9 (nonowned autos) can be used to provide liability coverage in a car rental situation. However, of these three symbols, only symbol 8 is typically used to provide physical damage coverage.

When symbol 8 is used for physical damage coverage, a rental car is treated in the same manner as a covered auto owned by the insured. The physical damage coverage would be primary unless the driver was included with the rental.

In addition to the selection of the proper covered vehicle symbol(s), you need to select among three possible physical damage cause of loss options:

- Physical damage comprehensive coverage: Includes losses by causes other than collision.
- Physical damage specified causes of loss coverage: Includes losses caused by fire, lightning, explosion, theft, windstorm, hail, earthquake, flood, mischief, or vandalism.
- Physical damage collision coverage: Includes loss resulting from collision with another object or overturn.

When symbol 8 and cause of loss coverage are selected, the BAP will provide you with primary physical damage coverage for rental cars. The BAP physical damage coverage insuring agreement states, "We will pay for 'loss' to a covered auto or its equipment under: comprehensive coverage / specified causes of loss coverage / collision coverage (depending on your selection)."

The BAP defines "loss" as "direct and accidental loss or damage" to a covered auto. On the basis of this definition, it would seem that the policy would pay only for direct damage to the vehicle. This could mean that indirect or consequential damages such as the rental car company's charge for loss of use or administrative fees would not be covered.

However, coverage for the insured's legal liability for loss of use fees can be included by endorsement to the policy. The coverage is limited to $15 per day with a maximum of $450. More recent policy forms may increase loss of use coverage for $20 per day with a $600 maximum. Even with this additional coverage, the per day limitation might not be sufficient to satisfy the rental company's loss of use claim.

There may also be other gaps between your financial responsibility for the rental vehicle and the physical damage coverage provided by your BAP including the following:

Electronic equipment

The physical damage coverage insuring agreement states that the policy will pay for loss to the covered auto *and its equipment.* But the policy fails to define "equipment," so that term will become subject to interpretation in the event of a loss.

There is also an exclusion in the policy that says, "We will not pay for loss to any of the following: (c) any electronic equipment, without regard to whether this equipment is permanently installed, that receives or transmits audio, visual, or data signals and that is not designed solely for the reproduction of sound."

By means of an exception to this exclusion, the policy goes on to indicate that sound reproduction equipment permanently installed in the vehicle is covered as is other electronic equipment "necessary for the normal operation of the covered auto or the monitoring of the covered auto's operating system."

Some insurers may interpret this exclusion to mean that other electronic equipment such as the satellite navigational devices found in many rental cars will not be covered under the BAP physical damage coverage. This exclusion may also preclude coverage for cellular phones even when permanently installed in the rental car.

Tires

The BAP also contains an exclusion that reads, "We will not pay for loss caused by or resulting from any of the following unless caused by other loss that is covered by this insurance: (b) blowouts, punctures, or other road damage to tires." So if a tire becomes damaged as a result of a collision loss (and you had selected collision coverage), the BAP will pay for it. If you simply run over a nail and puncture a tire, it will not.

Limits of insurance

The physical damage coverage section of the policy titled "Limits of Insurance" states, "The most we will pay for loss in any one accident is the lesser of: (1) the actual cash value of the damaged or stolen property at the time of the loss, or (2) the cost of repairing or replacing the damaged or stolen property with other property of like kind and quality."

In the event the rental company pursues a loss of turn-back claim for an amount above the vehicle's actual cash value, the BAP would not cover that amount and would leave your company financially responsible for the difference.

Deductible

Any claim paid under your BAP will be subject to the appropriate physical damage coverage deductible as listed on your policy declaration page.

Policy conditions

There is an important condition in the BAP titled "Duties in the Event of Accident, Claim, Suit, or Loss" that pertains to both liability and physical damage coverage.

This provision states, "In the event of an accident, claim, suit, or loss, you must give us or our authorized representative prompt notice of the accident or loss. Additionally, you or any other involved insured must assume no obligation, make no payment, or incur no expense without our consent, except at the insured's own cost. If there is a loss to a covered auto or its equipment, you must also ... permit us to inspect the covered auto and records proving the loss before its repair or disposition."

Several points need to be made. First, it is always a good idea to report all losses and accidents involving rental cars to your BAP insurer even if you believe that the rental company will ultimately handle any resultant claims. If the rental company changes its position at a later date and you are forced to report the claim to your insurer, there is always the possibility that the insurer could refuse to provide coverage on the basis of your violation of this policy condition.

It is also important that you do not make any payments to the rental company for damages to the rental car. If your insurer does not agree with the amount to which you committed, you could find yourself personally responsible for the difference.

Finally, providing your insurer with the opportunity to inspect the damaged rental car before it is repaired is certainly problematic when you don't control that property. But by promptly reporting the loss to your BAP insurer, you will be doing everything possible to comply with your responsibilities under the BAP.

chapter ten

Protection Provided by Other Insurance Policies

The previous chapters examined coverage that may be available under your personal and business auto policies to help protect you against your car rental risk exposures. What about any other insurance policies you may have? Is any coverage found under those polices?

Several other policies common to individuals and businesses will be discussed below in regards to potential rental car coverage.

COMMERCIAL GENERAL LIABILITY POLICY

Most companies purchase a commercial general liability (CGL) policy to provide coverage for their liability exposures. However, they should not look to their CGL policy for coverage for losses resulting from their use of rental cars.

The CGL provides bodily injury and property damage liability protection under coverage A of its policy form. The coverage A insuring agreement states that the insurer "will pay those sums that the insured becomes legally obligated to pay as damages because of bodily injury or property damage to which this insurance applies." It further expresses the insurer's "duty to defend the insured against any suit seeking those damages."

This broad insuring agreement does not indicate whether liability coverage might exist for your car rental exposure. A key phrase in the insuring agreement is "to which this insurance applies."

Coverage A consists of two parts: the insuring agreement and the exclusions. In order to determine what coverage A of the CGL does cover, it is necessary to understand what exposures are specifically excluded.

The auto liability exposure is addressed under exclusion G, aircraft, auto, or watercraft. This exclusion precludes coverage for "bodily injury or property damage arising out of the ownership, maintenance, use, or entrustment to others of any aircraft, auto, or watercraft owned or operated by or rented or loaned to any insured."

The CGL form defines "auto" as "a land motor vehicle, trailer, or semi-trailer designed for travel on public roads, including any attached machinery or equipment." Because a rental car would be considered "a land motor vehicle … designed for travel on public roads," there is no liability coverage for rental cars.

The exclusion also includes the language "or entrustment to others." This expands the effect of the exclusion beyond the usual "ownership, maintenance, or use" criteria. The purpose of this expansion of the exclusion is to prevent coverage for negligent entrustment situations.

Because the CGL is a liability policy, there is no property or physical damage coverage that could apply to damage to the rental car.

BUSINESS OWNER'S POLICY

Small- and medium-sized companies insure their businesses under a business owner's policy (BOP). A BOP provides both basic property and liability coverage under a package policy concept.

The property coverage form of the BOP clearly excludes coverage for damage to a rental car. Its insuring agreement states that the insurer "will pay for direct physical loss of or damage to covered property at the premises described in the declarations caused by or resulting from any covered cause of loss."

However, under the policy's property not covered section that follows, it states, "Covered property does not include aircraft, automobiles, motor trucks, and other vehicles subject to motor vehicle registration."

The liability coverage form of the BOP also contains a similar automobile exclusion. The policy's aircraft, auto, or watercraft exclusion states that the policy does not apply to "bodily injury or property damage arising out of the ownership, maintenance, use, or entrustment to others of any aircraft, auto, or watercraft owned or operated by or rented or loaned to any insured."

HOMEOWNER'S POLICY

The homeowner's policy is similar to the business owner's policy in that it features a package policy concept that includes both property and liability protection.

A homeowner's policy is also comparable to a BOP in its treatment of the automobile exposure. The property coverage part of the policy specifically excludes coverage for motor vehicles that are designed for travel on public roads and that are subject to motor vehicle registration. Therefore, the policy will not cover damage to the rental vehicle.

The liability coverage part of the policy excludes coverage "for bodily injury and property damage arising out of the ownership, maintenance, use, loading, or unloading of a motor vehicle owned, operated by, or rented or loaned to any insured." This exclusion eliminates coverage for your legal liability to others resulting from your operation of the rental car, as well as your liability to the rental company for damage to the vehicle.

Some homeowner's policies are also adding an entrustment exclusion to the liability section as a result of some court decisions relative to the auto exposure. For example, you rent a car and lend it to a friend who is not considered an authorized driver under the terms of the rental contract. The friend is involved in a serious accident while operating the rental car.

The car rental company considers this to be a violation of the rental contract and denies any extended liability protection that might otherwise be available to you. Neither you nor your friend has any personal or business auto coverage available.

Under this scenario, the only available liability coverage would be the limit provided by the rental company. (In most states, the rental company would have to provide the minimum financial responsibility limit in spite of the rental contract violation.)

Because of the severity of the resultant injuries, a creative plaintiff attorney representing the driver and passengers of the other vehicle wants to find some liability coverage beyond the low limit provided by the rental company. To do so, he seeks coverage under your homeowner's policy by alleging that you negligently entrusted the rental car to your friend, who he claims to be an incompetent driver.

Although your homeowner's policy contains an exclusion for the ownership, maintenance, or use of a motor vehicle, the attorney argues that your liability has nothing to do with the ownership, maintenance, or use of the vehicle but rather with your negligent entrustment of the vehicle. When entrustment is not specifically excluded under a homeowner's policy, some courts have agreed that coverage does exist for this type of exposure.

PERSONAL UMBRELLA POLICY

In recent years, more and more individuals have been purchasing personal umbrella policies to help protect their assets. They understand that the coverage limits under their basic personal auto and homeowner's policies might not be adequate in today's litigious society. In the event the limits of those policies were exhausted, you could find your personal assets at risk if not for the protection provided by a personal umbrella policy.

A personal umbrella policy provides a high limit of worldwide liability coverage over and above the coverage provided by your underlying auto and homeowner's policies. The policy limit is generally $1 million or higher.

The policy provides two principal types of coverage. For certain exposures, the umbrella policy provides excess coverage over and above your underlying coverage limits, such as the protection provided under your personal auto and homeowner's policies. For certain other exposures for which you may not have any underlying coverage, the umbrella policy "drops down" to provide primary coverage (often with a small retained limit).

Unlike some other common policy forms previously discussed, there is no "standard" personal umbrella policy form. As a result, there is a wider variance among insurance companies in the coverages and exclusions found in umbrella policies than found in other coverage lines. The policy provisions of the personal umbrella policy may differ in terms of what is specifically included in the coverage, what is specifically excluded from coverage, and what underlying policies and limits are required to be maintained in full force.

Because of these differences among personal umbrella policy forms, it is very important that you understand the extent of the coverage provided. If the provisions of the personal umbrella policy differ from those of your underlying policies, coverage gaps could result. For that reason, it is usually a good idea to purchase a personal umbrella policy from the same company that provides your personal auto and homeowner's coverage.

A personal umbrella policy is intended to provide high limits of liability protection to individuals and families. If you are traveling on business and are involved in an accident with your rental car, your policy might not cover you because of your business activity.

NAMED NONOWNER COVERAGE

Many car rental contracts contain language that shifts the primary liability responsibility to the renter whenever possible. In the event of an accident involving a rental car, the renter has to call upon his or her personal auto policy for liability protection.

If a renter does not own an automobile and has no personal auto insurance, the protection provided by the rental company becomes primary. However, the limit of liability protection provided by the rental company under this circumstance is quite low (usually equal to the state minimum financial responsibility requirement).

How do people who do not own an auto obtain higher limits of liability protection when renting a car? One option is to purchase the increased liability protection optional coverage offered by the rental company. This coverage will be later discussed in detail.

Another option is to purchase named nonowner coverage. This coverage is generally written as an endorsement to a personal auto policy and is intended for those people who do not own a car but regularly operate nonowned vehicles such as rental cars.

A named nonowner endorsement covers only the person specifically named in the endorsement. It does not automatically include coverage for a spouse or other household members. If coverage is needed for those individuals, they must also be specifically named in the endorsement.

The liability coverage provided under a named nonowner endorsement is excess to other applicable liability insurance. Because of the shifting language contained in many car rental contracts, the same issues that apply to the primacy issue will also apply here.

When the rental company does provide primary liability protection, it is generally limited and may not be sufficient. Purchasing named nonowner coverage with high limits can solve that problem. Named nonowner coverage can also satisfy the underlying insurance requirement of a personal umbrella policy for those who don't own a car.

COVERAGE PROVIDED BY OTHER POLICIES

Other risk exposures you face when renting, such as your medical expenses resulting from an accident and loss to your personal property, may also be covered by other insurance you have. That topic will be discussed later in the "Other Optional Protection Plans" chapter.

chapter eleven

Protection Provided by Your Credit Cards

If you ever listen to other customers while waiting in line at the rental counter, you'll probably hear some refuse the loss damage waiver offered by the rental company and tell the rental agent that their credit card covers them. Although these people may be partially correct, few fully understand the extent of protection provided. Many believe that the coverage provided is more comprehensive than it actually is.

Why do customers think that relying on the protection provided by their credit card is sufficient? Consider one advertisement used by a credit card company to promote its car rental insurance benefit, which stated, in part:

"Relax and enjoy the ride! Because when you use (our card) to pick up and pay for a rental auto, you're covered."

Or one used by another credit card company in listing its benefits:

"Auto rental insurance at no additional cost."

Messages such as these lead some car rental customers to believe that all of their insurance needs will be met by their credit cards. Unfortunately, many may be disappointed in the event a loss occurs. Although the coverage provided by credit cards can be a valuable benefit, there are many restrictions and limitations that could leave you financially responsible for damages that you thought would be covered.

Although there are differences in benefits in the various credit card programs currently available, the following discussion should provide a fairly comprehensive overview of what you need to know before relying upon credit card coverage when renting a car.

The information that follows provides a summary of common credit card insurance provisions, but they may vary by company. There is no such thing as "standard" coverage, so you should obtain and review a copy of the complete summary of benefits issued by your particular credit card company. After reviewing that summary, you should contact the credit card company for clarification of any specific questions that remain.

TYPES OF CREDIT CARDS PROVIDING PROTECTION

Car rental coverage is not offered with all credit cards. This benefit has generally been limited to card programs offered by American Express and Diners Club as well as the Gold and/or Platinum cards of Visa and MasterCard, although it is gradually expanding to cards below the premium level. Many business or corporate card programs offered by these companies also receive some level of car rental coverage.

Don't assume that all credit cards provide similar protection or any protection at all for that matter. If owning a credit card that provides car rental insurance is important to you, you can obtain preliminary information about the level of benefits provided from the Internet Web sites of various card companies.

After you narrow your search to a couple of companies, you can contact each to request a complete copy of the plan's terms and conditions.

TYPE OF COVERAGE

Confusion sometimes exists about the type of coverage provided under credit card plans. One common misconception is that the car rental insurance plans offered by credit card companies include liability protection. They do not include liability coverage, nor do they provide no-fault insurance, uninsured motorist insurance, or other coverage for injuries to third parties or to occupants of the rental vehicle.

What type of coverage do these credit cards provide? This coverage is intended to provide coverage for damage to or theft of the rental car. Subject to the terms and conditions of the particular credit card program, the coverage helps protect you against the financial risk for damage to the rental vehicle you assume under the rental contract.

There are limitations to the credit card coverage that might still leave you financially responsible, at least in part. Some of the limitations often found in these plans include:

- There is often a limit of liability in terms the amount of direct damage that the card covers. Depending on the card, that limit may be $50,000, $75,000, or $100,000. If you use a card with a $50,000 limit, that might not be adequate to pay for a total loss of a more expensive rental vehicle.
- Some cards do not cover the rental company's loss of use claim. If the rental company pursues recovery of its loss of use damages, you could remain financially responsible.
- Most cards do not cover the rental company's claim for administrative fees. Again, you could become personally responsible.

Some of the cards include some ancillary coverage for loss to personal property and medical expenses for the renter and occupants of the rental vehicle. This coverage provides relatively low limits comparable to those provided under the personal accident insurance and personal effects coverage offered by the rental company.

WHO IT COVERS

In order to receive rental car insurance coverage under a credit card program, the card must be issued in your name, and the rental must also be in your name. Only you and other authorized drivers of the rental car will be covered in the event of loss.

HOW TO OBTAIN COVERAGE

In order for credit card coverage to apply, you must:

- Use your credit card to open the rental contract.
- Decline loss damage waiver (LDW), collision damage waiver (CDW), or any other option designed to cover damage to the rental car that is offered by the rental company.

- Use your credit card to pay for the entire rental transaction when you return the rental car. You cannot use your card to open the rental transaction and then use another method of payment (cash, other credit card, etc.) at closing. The credit card providing the rental insurance must be used throughout the rental transaction for coverage to apply.

Your failure to meet any of these conditions could void any coverage that would otherwise be provided by the card.

WHEN COVERAGE APPLIES

Coverage for damage to the rental car is generally in effect from the time you take possession of the vehicle until the time you return it to the rental company.

Some credit card companies limit the length of time that coverage will apply. Coverage is often limited to periods ranging from between 15 and 30 consecutive days. (For example, coverage may be limited to a maximum of 15 consecutive days when renting in the United States and 31 consecutive days when renting out of the country.) Coverage will be declined if a loss occurs beyond the maximum time limit.

You may not be able to circumvent this limit by extending your original rental contract and entering into a new contract or renting a different car from the same company. Some cards require a 72-hour period to pass from the time the original vehicle was returned before benefits will again apply.

You may be able to avoid this 72-hour requirement by renting from a different rental company. Card companies may also waive this restriction if you rent another car from the same company but in a different city that is a specified number of miles from the original location.

COVERAGE TERRITORY

Most car rental insurance plans offered by credit card companies provide coverage on a worldwide basis. However, the benefits may differ for losses outside the United States.

Some cards also include territorial restrictions in some parts of the world. Some plans exclude coverage for vehicles rented in countries such as Ireland, Israel, Jamaica, Australia, and New Zealand.

When you plan to rent a car outside of the United States, you should ask your credit card company whether your rental will be covered in your destination country.

PRIMARY VS. SECONDARY COVERAGE

The car rental insurance provided by credit card plans may be either primary or secondary. If primary, it will provide coverage for damage to the rental car regardless of any other protection you might have available. If it is secondary, coverage applies only after you have exhausted all other available coverage, including your personal or business auto insurance.

For credit card holders who are residents of the United States, coverage generally applies on a secondary basis for rentals in the United States. This means that the coverage will pay only for what is not covered under your other insurance policies. If your insurance company pays for the damage to the rental car, the credit card coverage might pay for damages not covered by your insurance such as the rental company's loss of use. It may also pay the amount of any deductible for which you are responsible.

If you have no other insurance coverage or protection available to you, the credit card coverage would then become primary and would pay for the full amount of the damage, subject to other restrictions and limitations of your credit card plan.

There are some credit cards that provide primary coverage for U.S. rentals, regardless of the availability of other insurance. These are often the prestige or premium versions of the cards offered by credit card companies. Primary coverage benefits may also be offered as a benefit to corporate customers who do not want to involve their business auto insurance company.

Outside of the United States, coverage is almost always provided on a primary basis. This may not represent as great a benefit as it might initially appear. The reality is that most U.S. cardholders will not have any personal insurance that applies outside of this country, so offering "primary" coverage is a somewhat hollow benefit. Without any other available coverage, a plan providing secondary coverage would become primary anyway.

TYPES OF RENTAL VEHICLES COVERED

Credit card coverage is usually provided when the following vehicles are rented:
- Private passenger automobiles, unless specifically excluded
- Minivans and sports utility vehicles designed to accommodate eight occupants or fewer (some plans allow vehicles that can accommodate up to nine occupants).

TYPES OF VEHICLES EXCLUDED

The following are vehicles generally excluded under credit card plans:

- "Expensive automobiles" that are sometimes defined as having a manufacturer's suggested retail price (MSRP) greater than a specified amount (i.e., $50,000)
- "Exotic automobiles," which may include cars such as Ferrari, Lamborghini, Maserati, Porsche, Mercedes, BMW, Rolls Royce, Chevrolet Corvette, Plymouth Prowler, and others
- Antique autos (more than 20 years old and not manufactured for 10 years)
- Trucks, pickups, and cargo vans
- Customized and full-sized vans
- Vehicles rented for commercial purposes
- Motorcycles, RVs, and off-road vehicles
- Customized or modified vehicles

If you have any question about whether the vehicle you intend to rent will be covered or excluded under the terms of your credit card coverage, you should always check with your credit card company prior to rental.

OTHER EXCLUSIONS

Credit card car rental insurance provides coverage for direct damage to the rental car, theft of the rental car, and reasonable loss of use charged by the rental company. But there are a number of exclusions contained in most credit card rental insurance policies of which you need to be aware.

Losses caused by or resulting from the following are generally not covered by credit card rental insurance plans:

- Use of the vehicle by a driver who is not authorized by the rental company, even when using the vehicle with your permission
- Operation of the rental vehicle while under the influence of an intoxicant
- Use or operation of the rental vehicle in violation of any other use restriction listed on the rental contract
- Injury to any person
- Damage to any vehicle or any other property other than the rental car
- Your legal liability to any party or entity other than the rental company
- Damage to the rental car due to wear and tear, gradual deterioration, or mechanical breakdown

- Damage to tires (flats or blowouts) unless such damage is the result of a covered loss (such as collision)
- Unauthorized off-road operation of the rental car
- Use of the rental car for hire or commercial purposes
- Depreciation, diminution of value, or administrative fees charged by the rental company
- Theft of or damage to unlocked vehicles or vehicles with the keys left in them
- Loss due to confiscation by authorities
- Losses due to war or any other hostility
- Losses resulting from illegal activity
- Subsequent damage resulting from a failure to protect the vehicle after a loss

If you plan to rely upon the coverage provided by your credit card when renting, you should contact your card company for a complete list of exclusions prior to renting.

FILING A CLAIM

Claim reporting procedures vary by company. Some card companies will deal directly with the rental company while others may require that you first pay for the vehicle damages yourself and then file a claim to obtain reimbursement.

Most people would rather have the credit card company deal directly with the rental company than be "stuck in the middle" between the two. That position can become uncomfortable when the credit card company asks for additional documentation such as itemized repair bills or loss of use justification and you have to request that information from the car rental company. Imagine having to go back and forth a number of times before the card company is satisfied. If you wish to avoid that type of administrative burden, search for a credit card company that will deal directly with the rental company and leave you out of the process.

If you have an accident in or damage your rental car, it is critical that you fully understand the reporting requirements of your credit card company. If you do not satisfy those requirements within the specified time frame, your claim could be denied.

Although reporting requirements vary by car rental insurance plan, some of the more common requirements include the following:

- Credit card plans often give you a deadline for filing the initial report of your claim. That deadline is usually 20 to 30 days from the date the loss occurs. You may be able to satisfy this requirement by phoning a toll-free accident reporting number listed on your coverage summary or using the card company's online claim reporting service.
- At some point, you will be required to complete and sign a claim report form. Again, you may have a deadline (generally between 60 and 90 days) for completing the form and returning it along with the requested documentation.
- In addition to the completed claim form, the credit card company may require that you provide copies of your rental contract, itemized repair bill, police report, and photos of the damaged vehicle. If your credit card coverage is secondary, you may also be required to provide documentation (or at least a notarized statement) verifying that you have no other available insurance or that your other insurance will not cover the claim.
- If you cannot provide all requested documentation within the required time frame, you will be required to submit as much as is available to you at that time. The insurance company may give you a final deadline (usually between 180 and 365 days) to submit all remaining documents.

You must adhere to all reporting requirements and deadlines in order for your claim to be considered. The credit card company may deny your claim if you fail to comply.

QUESTIONS TO ASK YOUR CREDIT CARD COMPANY BEFORE RENTING

If you do decide to use the car rental insurance benefit provided by your credit card company, be sure to fully understand all provisions of the plan and review the coverage summary provided by the card company. (The summary is usually sent to you at the time you obtain your credit cards. Updates and revisions may also be sent periodically.)

After reviewing the coverage summary, you should then contact the card company's customer service department with any questions. Some may include:

- Is the location where you will be renting covered under the plan?
- Is the vehicle you plan to rent covered?
- Will coverage extend through the entire duration of the rental period?

- Will coverage apply on a primary or secondary basis?
- Will additional drivers be covered?
- In the event of loss, will the insurance company pay damages directly to the rental company, or will you have to pay them and seek reimbursement?
- What number should you call to report a claim?
- Will the plan cover the rental company's claim for loss of use? (Many plans do cover "reasonable" loss of use if the rental company can prove its loss. But be aware that if the credit card company refuses to pay the entire loss of use claim, the rental company may try to collect directly from you.)
- Will the plan also cover the rental company's administrative fees? (Most plans do not, which means that you still might be held responsible.)
- Are there any restrictions on the manner in which you intend to use the vehicle (i.e., vacation, business, etc.)?
- Are there any other restrictions or limitations of which you should be aware?

The coverage for damage to the rental car provided under a credit card plan can be a valuable benefit if you have no other coverage available. It can also supplement your other coverage by at least providing reimbursement for your deductible.

As an educated car rental customer, you need to understand the requirements and limitations of your credit card plan. If you don't, you could be in for a surprise if you ever have a claim.

chapter twelve

Loss Damage Waiver

Loss damage waiver (LDW) is an optional protection product that waives the renter's financial responsibility for damage to the rental vehicle. It is offered by rental companies for an additional daily charge.

The rental industry goes to great lengths to convey the message that LDW is not insurance. To even indirectly imply that it is insurance could subject the companies to scrutiny by the various state insurance departments—something that the industry wants to avoid because such regulation would probably require companies to actuarially justify the rate charged to customers.

LDW is the descendant of collision damage waiver (CDW), an earlier version of the waiver. CDW was more restrictive in that it waived the renter's responsibility for vehicle damage only when the damage resulted from a collision with another vehicle or object.

The broader LDW option relieves the renter from responsibility for damage that results from virtually any cause, including vandalism, theft, and glass breakage. But it is important to understand that a violation of the terms of the rental contract can void this protection, even when selected and paid for by the renter.

Although it is becoming increasingly rare, some companies still offer the earlier CDW version. However, many states now require a complete waiver of a renter's responsibility for vehicle damage when any type of waiver is purchased. When renting a car and considering the purchase of the waiver offered by the rental company, be sure you understand whether it is being sold as LDW or CDW. The difference could be rather significant in the event the rental car is damaged.

STATE REGULATION OF LDW

Although LDW has for the most part escaped the close review of insurance department regulators, it has been the subject of state legislation. At this time, approximately one-half of the states regulate the sale of LDW to some degree.

In the past, a few states had LDW laws that were quite extreme. For example, Illinois and New York had laws that limited the renter's financial responsibility for loss of or damage to the rental vehicle. That responsibility was limited to $200 in Illinois and $100 in New York. Because of this limitation of the renter's responsibility, these laws did not allow the sale of any type of waiver in those states.

These laws were extremely detrimental to the rental industry. Customers didn't need to exercise much care for the rental car because the laws limited their financial exposure. Because the rental companies were prohibited from seeking recovery of their loss from the customer (even when the customer was clearly responsible for the damage), they sustained significant losses.

The law in Illinois was changed in 1997 to allow rental companies to recover damages from customers. The maximum amount recoverable is still limited to an amount less than the full value of the vehicle, but the new law is clearly more beneficial to the rental industry than the former law. With the abolishment of the $200 cap, the Illinois law also allows the rental companies to sell LDW so customers can protect themselves against the financial responsibility of vehicle damage.

The New York law was changed in March of 2003. It also allows rental companies to recover their vehicle damage amounts from renters. But unlike the Illinois law, companies in New York can pursue the full amount of the damages. Companies in New York are also now allowed to offer LDW to their customers.

LDW statutes are usually limited to passenger vehicles. Trucks and other cargo-carrying vehicles (including cargo vans) are generally not subject to LDW laws. The issues addressed by state LDW laws are rather diverse. Some issues pertaining to LDW may be regulated in some states but not in others.

Most LDW laws are somewhat consistent in that they usually address the following:

- **Specific LDW notice on the rental contract:** The most common provision of LDW laws requires that the terms of the rental contract clearly describe the renter's responsibility for vehicle damage as well as the level of protection provided by LDW.
- **Acceptance or rejection:** The contract must have an area where the renter must sign or initial acceptance or rejection of LDW.
- **Pricing:** Some states limit the daily rate that can be charged for LDW.
- **Method of calculating the amount of damages:** The laws sometimes specify the manner in which the rental company can charge the customer for repairs (i.e., on the basis of actual costs including available discounts, etc.).
- **Renter's level of responsibility:** Some LDW laws require that the purchase of LDW must waive the full amount of the renter's responsibility for damage.
- **Use restrictions that can void LDW if violated:** Some states limit the use restrictions the rental companies can use to void LDW if violated.

TYPES OF LDW

The rental industry offers several different types of LDW plans that can vary by company and sometimes even by type of vehicle or rental location within the same company. Some of those variations include the following:

Full LDW

This waiver relieves the renter of all responsibility for loss of or damage to the rental vehicle (including loss of use and administrative fees) regardless of whether the damage results from collision, theft, vandalism, forces of nature, or other causes. It applies up to the full value of the vehicle without any deductible or other charge (other than the cost of the waiver) to the renter.

Partial or limited LDW

A partial waiver limits the renter's responsibility to a stated amount as listed on the rental agreement, such as $500 or $1,000. The renter is responsible for loss or damage up to that amount, and any damage above the stated amount is waived. This type of waiver is comparable to having a deductible under a personal auto policy.

Deductible protection LDW
This waiver works in the opposite way as the limited waiver. With this waiver, the renter's financial responsibility for vehicle damage is waived up to a specified amount. The renter is then responsible for all damage above the stated amount. This waiver is intended for customers who have other personal or business insurance but with a large deductible. The waiver frees the renter from responsibility up to the policy deductible amount. Because the renter's insurer pays for the remainder of the damage above the deductible amount, the renter avoids all responsibility.

LDW offered by outside companies
Probably as a result of the profitability of selling LDW, some outside vendors also offer a LDW product to car rental customers. Several insurance companies are currently offering the product through various travel providers and sources.

One Internet travel company offers LDW to customers who make car rental reservations through its Web site. Interestingly, this places the company in direct competition with the car rental companies that fulfill the reservations.

Customers should use caution when buying LDW from anyone other than the car rental company. They may buy it assuming that they will be fully protected only to later find that there could be gaps in their coverage. The LDW offered directly by the rental companies may cost a little more, but you will probably be less likely to experience a problem if you damage the rental car.

LDW EXCLUSIONS
The protection available under LDW may be voided, leaving you fully responsible for all loss of or damage to the rental vehicle, including loss of use and related expenses, if:
- The vehicle is operated by someone other than the renter or other authorized driver (as defined by the rental contract)
- The vehicle is used in violation of a prohibited use listed on the rental contract

These restrictions may appear to operate in a similar manner as the exclusions listed in a personal auto policy. However, the rental contract use restrictions are generally more severe than with a personal auto policy. For example, your personal auto policy will extend coverage to virtually anyone

128

operating your vehicle with your permission. A rental contract requires that only authorized drivers (as defined by the contract) operate the vehicle. Simply having your permission is not sufficient.

Another example involves driving under the influence of intoxicants. If you drive your own car while under the influence and have an accident, your insurer will probably still afford coverage and repair your car. If you damage your rental car while intoxicated, you will have voided the LDW and will be held fully responsible for all damage.

COST

LDW is available for an additional daily charge that is payable for each full or partial rental day. The daily rate for LDW can vary by company, location, and type of vehicle, but it typically ranges between $5 and $18 per day. When the daily rate is found to be low in the range, it is usually because of state regulation.

In contrast to the physical damage coverage (collision and comprehensive) provided under a personal auto policy, the LDW daily rate is typically not actuarially based. Instead, it is highly dependant on competitive factors. It is not uncommon to find most car rental companies charging nearly the same LDW rate in a particular location.

This helps explain why the rental industry goes to great lengths to avoid referring to LDW as insurance. This avoidance of pricing regulation by state insurance departments has been the subject of much criticism in the past, with the principal complaint that it has been grossly overpriced.

A strong case could be made in support of that argument. Consider that at a daily rate of $15, the annualized cost of LDW would be $5,475! This annualized cost is for physical damage protection only and doesn't even include liability coverage.

The rental industry's response has always been that the physical risk to their vehicles is much greater than that faced by personal auto insurance carriers. The nature of the rental business requires companies to accept customers without the opportunity to underwrite the risk to the degree that insurers are able to do.

Considering its high cost, why would a rental customer want to consider purchasing LDW? There are a number of reasons why a customer may want or not want to purchase LDW:

Rental contract vs. insurance policy provisions

The terms of the rental contract are often more restrictive than the conditions of an auto insurance policy. If you allow an unauthorized driver to operate the rental car or in some other way violate a use restriction, you may void the LDW and be left without coverage.

On the other hand, an auto policy may have certain restrictions (such as an excluded driver) that you can circumvent by purchasing LDW. If the individual who is excluded under your auto policy qualifies as an additional authorized driver, you can obtain protection that your auto policy wouldn't provide.

Some auto insurance policies may not provide coverage while operating a rental car. Personal auto policies sometimes have limitations in regards to the operation of rental cars. Others have exclusions for business use. If you are not sure whether your policy will protect you, purchasing LDW might be the safe choice.

Causes of loss

LDW generally relieves you of all financial responsibility for damage to the rental car, regardless of how the damage happens. In order to have "full" physical damage coverage under your auto policy, it must include both collision and comprehensive (or other than collision) coverage in order for you to be protected.

Losses not covered by personal insurance

If you are involved in an accident while operating a rental car, you may find that your own auto insurance does not cover the entire loss. You need to be certain that your policy will cover the full value of the rental car, as well as the rental company's loss of use and administrative fees.

Rental companies may also pursue a claim for diminution of value, which may not be covered by personal insurance. Your insurance company may also refuse to pay for new replacement parts if its normal repair policy calls for the use of used parts.

If any portion of the claim made by the rental company is not covered by your own insurance, you could remain personally responsible and face some unanticipated costs.

Your duties after an accident

Your personal auto policy requires that you report accidents immediately and make the vehicle available for the insurance company's inspection. In most cases, the rental company is going to begin repairs immediately and not wait for your insurer to arrange such inspection. If your insurance company has any problem with the appraisal and cost prepared by the rental company, you could become responsible for any portion of the repairs your insurer refuses to pay.

Primary vs. excess protection

If you use your own insurance, there might be some question about whether it should respond on a primary basis, especially if you have other potential sources of protection available. Although the various insurance companies are arguing about responsibility, the rental company will be pressuring you to pay its claim.

In some cases, the rental company might even charge the repair amount to your credit card (if permitted by law). This could affect your available credit limit. If it takes a long time to resolve the question of which insurance applies first, you could be "out of pocket" for the repair bill.

When you purchase LDW, the question of primacy is no longer an issue. Your responsibility for damage is waived regardless of whether you have any other insurance available to you.

Total cost

There is no question that LDW is expensive. But if you rent infrequently, or on a short-term basis, purchasing LDW can be a smart financial decision.

If you rely on your own coverage, you'll probably be responsible for paying your policy deductible. If that deductible is relatively large (for example $500 or $1,000), spending an extra $10 to $15 per day for LDW might be worthwhile.

You could also face a premium increase, or possibly even cancellation of your personal policy, if you file a claim. If you decide to purchase the LDW protection, your insurance company probably won't have to get involved.

In conclusion, only you can decide whether to purchase the rental company's LDW. After carefully weighing all of these factors, as well as your tolerance for risk, it becomes your job to make an educated decision.

Unfortunately, many car rental customers fail to carefully evaluate these factors in making their decisions. A 2002 survey performed by the Progressive group of insurance companies indicated that 19% of car rental customers always purchased LDW and another 19% bought it occasionally.

Of those that bought LDW, 63% indicated that they did so because they desired the extra protection. But 24% said that they purchased it because they were unsure whether their personal policies provided enough coverage, and another 8% bought it only because they felt pressured by the rental agent.

The unfortunate conclusion is that many travelers don't know enough about renting a car to be able to make this purchase decision with confidence. Nearly one-third accepted the LDW only because they felt pressured or were unsure whether they needed it.

The decision must be yours and yours alone. The rental agent doesn't know what type of insurance you have and can't really help you decide. The rental company cannot require that you purchase LDW. The current state regulations that apply to LDW make it clear that LDW is meant to be an optional protection product. If your car rental company makes its purchase a condition of rental, you should seek out a different company.

chapter thirteen

Increased Liability Protection

Most rental car companies offer some form of optional excess liability insurance that allows renters to increase the limit of liability protection they have available to them while operating the rental vehicle. In contrast to LDW, this protection is insurance that is often underwritten by independent insurance companies.

Increased liability protection is offered under a number of different names. Depending on which car rental company you're doing business with, it might be called:

- Additional liability insurance (ALI)
- Extended liability protection (ELP)
- Liability insurance supplement (LIS)
- Supplemental liability insurance (SLI)
- Supplemental liability protection (SLP)

Because the variance in terms used throughout the rental industry can become somewhat confusing, we will refer to this optional protection simply as increased liability protection throughout this discussion.

WHAT INCREASED LIABILITY PROTECTION COVERS

Increased liability protection allows renters to obtain a high limit of liability against third-party bodily injury and property damage claims that result from their use of the rental vehicle.

WHO INCREASED LIABILITY PROTECTION COVERS

This protection applies to the renter and other authorized operators of the rental vehicle. The increased liability protection insurance policy usually defines "renter" and "authorized driver" in a manner consistent with the rental contract.

LIMIT OF LIABILITY

The limit of liability is usually the difference between the limit of liability protection provided under the terms of the rental contract (the state financial responsibility limit) and $1 million combined single limit per occurrence. The result is that the cumulative liability limit available to the renter or authorized driver is $1 million combined single limit when increased liability protection is purchased. Combined single limit (or CSL) refers to the maximum amount that will be paid for the sum of all claims resulting from a single accident. The effect is that the purchase of increased liability protection provides the renter with liability protection up to $1 million for all claims resulting from an accident.

PRIMARY LIABILITY PROTECTION

Depending on individual state law and the terms of the rental contract, a rental car company may provide renters with either primary liability protection or secondary liability protection. However, when increased liability protection is purchased, rental companies usually agree to provide the renter with primary liability protection up to the applicable state financial responsibility limit.

There are a few rental companies that choose to maintain a secondary liability position when allowed to do so even when the renter purchases increased liability protection. As a result, other personal or business liability protection or insurance available to the renter would apply first, and the optional increased liability protection would then increase the renter's protection up to $1 million.

134

BENEFITS OF PURCHASING INCREASED LIABILITY PROTECTION

The renter receives two significant benefits when increased liability protection is purchased:

- The renter obtains a high limit ($1 million CSL) of liability protection.
- The liability protection is primary to any other protection or insurance available to the renter. As a result, the renter probably won't need to involve his or her personal insurance carrier unless the total value of all claims resulting from an accident exceeds $1 million.

The second benefit applies only when the car rental company agrees to provide primary liability protection whenever increased liability protection is purchased.

COST

Increased liability protection is offered at an additional charge that applies for each full or partial rental day. The daily cost may vary by company and location and is usually in the $8.00 to $14.00 range.

EXCLUSIONS

Other exclusions typically found in an increased liability protection policy include:

- Operation of the rental vehicle by an unauthorized driver
- Operation of the rental vehicle by the renter or other authorized driver in violation of the terms of the rental contract
- Obtaining a rental vehicle by fraud or misrepresentation
- Causing bodily injury to the renter, other authorized drivers, or members of their families who reside in their households

Increased liability protection is offered only at rental locations in the United States. Coverage applies when the rental vehicle is operated in the United States or in Canada (when the rental originates in the United States). These policies generally exclude coverage if the rental vehicle is driven into Mexico.

Insurance companies providing increased liability protection try to make their policy terms and conditions as consistent as possible with those contained in the rental contract. So if you violate the terms of the rental contract and void any liability protection the rental company would otherwise provide, you probably won't receive any protection under the increased liability protection policy either.

UNINSURED MOTORIST AND UNDERINSURED MOTORIST COVERAGE

Many increased liability protection policies do not include uninsured motorist (UM), underinsured motorist (UIM), personal injury protection (PIP), and other first party no-fault coverages. However, a few rental companies offer increased liability protection that does include some limited uninsured/underinsured motorist coverage (UM/UIM), usually up to $100,000 CSL.

When an increased liability protection policy does include UM/UIM coverage, the benefits apply to individuals physically occupying the rental vehicle while the vehicle is operated by the renter or authorized driver and who suffer bodily injury or death caused by a negligent uninsured motorist, a negligent underinsured motorist, or a negligent hit and run driver. The maximum amount of protection available per accident is usually $100,000. The $100,000 limit includes any UM/UIM protection required by state law or provided under the terms of the rental contract and coverage available under increased liability protection.

The exclusion "for bodily injury to the renter, other authorized drivers or members of their families who reside in their households" does not apply to UM/UIM benefits.

WHO SHOULD PURCHASE INCREASED LIABILITY PROTECTION

Increased liability protection is intended for renters who:

- May not have any other personal or business liability protection available to them while operating a rental vehicle. In the absence of other liability insurance, the only protection available to renters who do not purchase increased liability protection is limited to the minimum state financial responsibility limit provided by the rental contract.
- Do have other liability insurance available but desire a higher limit. Some renters might feel comfortable with a lower liability limit on their personal auto policy but want all the liability protection they can get when operating an unfamiliar rental vehicle in a strange location.

- Have other personal or business auto liability protection available but don't want to have to make a claim against their personal insurance policy in the event of an accident. In addition to the high limit, the increased liability protection products offered by most rental companies provide primary protection.

FILING A CLAIM

If you are involved in an accident with your rental car, you should immediately report it to the rental company. If you do so, it is usually not necessary to file a separate claim report with the insurance company providing the increased liability protection. The rental company (or its claim handler) will usually do so on your behalf. However, it is recommended that you confirm this with your rental company to ensure that you maintain compliance with all accident-reporting requirements.

Increased liability protection can be of considerable value to some renters, especially those with no other liability coverage available or with low limits on their personal policies. With the higher chances of becoming involved in an accident with a rental car than in your own car, you may desire the extra protection, if only for peace of mind.

However, increased liability protection is not inexpensive, so the added protection comes at a price. For that reason, it is recommended that customers determine the extent of liability protection available to them, as well as their level of risk tolerance, before deciding whether to select this option with their next rental.

chapter fourteen

Other Optional Protection Plans

Loss damage waiver and increased liability protection are by far the rental industry's most popular optional protection plans. However, many car rental companies also offer their customers a variety of other optional plans.

Some feel that these optional protection plans are not needed and are a waste of your travel dollars. But there are situations in which some of these optional coverages could prove to be of significant value to you.

How do you determine whether you need to buy any of these optional protection plans? The only way you can arrive at the correct decision is to be as prepared as possible before you reach the rental counter. In order to do so, you need to:

- Have a general understanding of each of the insurance product or plan that will be offered
- Know whether your other personal and/or business insurance policies provide comparable coverage
- Be ready to ask questions about the details of the particular protection products offered by the rental company

The following discussion will provide you with a general description of the plans most commonly offered. It will also describe the types of policies you may already have that provide similar protection and explain that it is your responsibility to contact your insurance agent and ask what might be available under your policies; the rental agent won't be able to answer that question for you. Finally, it will help you evaluate your exposures and suggest the questions you need to ask the rental agent about the specific plans offered by the company.

Rental companies offer these optional coverages mainly for two reasons. First, the protection offered is needed by some renters. When that is the case, the coverage can be very valuable. Contrary to some opinion, these plans (1) are not solely designed to "rip off" customers, (2) do provide legitimate insurance protection, and (3) have provided many customers with benefits after they have losses. These plans must be filed with state insurance departments and are closely regulated.

The other reason these plans are offered is that they do generate significant revenue for the rental companies. In some cases, the amount of optional insurance sales could mean the difference between profit and loss for the company. The sale of optional protection also produces a significant portion of the rental agent's income in the form of commissions, incentives, and bonuses.

Because it is in the financial interest of both the rental company and the agent to convince you to purchase this protection, rental agents can use some pretty strong sales techniques to get you to buy. They know that most renters are ill prepared to make these decisions and many will purchase them simply out of fear rather than refusing them and taking the risk that they might have been needed.

Being unprepared to make this purchase decision can be a real dilemma for rental customers. Some decline the optional protection only to discover after a loss that they have no other comparable coverage available. Others accept the options, later learn that they did already have other protection available, and feel that they were duped into buying something they didn't really need.

It becomes your responsibility to do some homework before you rent. Understanding what protection each of these plans provides is the first step. You then must determine whether you already have similar coverage available to you. If not, you then need to evaluate whether buying the optional coverage is a risk you want to assume.

The optional protections plans offered by car rental companies will differ to some degree. You should not rely totally on the descriptions that follow because the plans may not all be identical. These descriptions are solely intended to provide you with a general overview of the most common plans.

HOW TO OBTAIN OPTIONAL PROTECTION PRODUCTS

Some rental car companies offer their optional protection plans to the renter at the time a reservation is made. Others do not make the offer until the renter appears at the rental location to execute the rental agreement and pick up the vehicle. Either way, once you inform the rental agent of your decision to purchase one or more of the protection plans, an entry will be made into the rental system documenting your selection. At the time you pick up your vehicle and execute the rental agreement, you will be asked to initial the agreement to signify your acceptance or rejection of each plan that was offered.

It is becoming more common for rental companies to provide frequent renters with paperless transactions in which they bypass the rental counter completely. In those cases, the company requires the renter to enroll by completing an application or enrollment form. That form provides customers with the opportunity to include any optional protection plans in their rental profiles. When you enroll in a company's frequent rental program of this type, the optional protection plan selections you make will apply to every rental unless you notify the company of your desire to change your profile. Requests for such changes are often required to be in writing.

HOW TO CONFIRM THAT THE RENTAL COMPANY WILL PROVIDE THE OPTIONAL INSURANCE PRODUCTS YOU SELECTED

Rental contracts often contain a space in which the renter has to initial the acceptance or rejection of each optional insurance product. The contract will also list an additional daily charge for each optional product selected.

You will be provided with a copy of your rental contract at the beginning of your rental period. You should check to make sure that you initialed your acceptance or rejection of the optional protection plans in the proper manner on the rental contract. You should also make certain that the additional daily charge for the plan also appears on the contract. If you make a claim, the insurance company will review a copy of the rental contract to verify that you both accepted and paid for the coverage.

If your rental contract does not clearly show that you purchased the coverage, the insurance company will not honor your claim. The argument that you requested the coverage but the rental agent forgot to list it on the contract will not get you very far.

CHANGING YOUR MIND AFTER LEAVING THE RENTAL FACILITY

You will not be allowed to make any changes in your optional protection plan selections after the rental period begins. Most companies require that you return to the rental facility, close out the current contract, and execute a new one.

To allow a customer to simply call in changes in plan selections is not acceptable to the insurers of these optional protection plans. Requiring a new contract precludes a customer from calling in after a loss occurs and adding the suddenly needed protection.

FILING A CLAIM

If you suffer a loss that might be covered by one of the optional protection plans you selected, immediately contact the rental location from which you rented the vehicle. You'll be provided with a claim form to complete and submit to the insurance company.

Be sure to follow the instructions provided with the claim form and include all required documentation supporting your claim when you submit it. Most plans require that you include a copy of your rental contract with your claim form. The form may also instruct you to provide bills, receipts, a police report, or other such documentation. Failure to do so will result in the insurance company having to recontact you and could delay the handling of your claim.

Upon receipt of your claim form, the insurer will review your rental contract to verify that you actually purchased its coverage. The insurer will then review the submitted documentation and let you know whether any additional information is required. If so requested, you should to respond back to the insurance company as quickly as possible.

Required claim reporting procedures may vary, so be sure that you immediately contact your rental company after sustaining a loss to determine exactly what you need to do. Failure to follow the stated claim procedures could possibly jeopardize your claim.

Some plans require that you submit your claim form to the insurance carrier providing the coverage within 20 days. For others, this reporting requirement is 30 days.

VIOLATION OF THE RENTAL CONTRACT

Your violation of a provision of the rental contract can void any coverage that would be otherwise provided by an optional protection plan. Even if you select and pay for an optional protection plan, the insurance company could refuse to provide coverage if you violate any of the terms of the contract.

PROTECTION PRODUCT BROCHURES

Most states require the rental company to provide the customer with information describing the basic terms and conditions of the coverage. This requirement is often satisfied by means of a product brochure or other similar material.

The brochure must provide an overview of the coverage, including relevant limitations and exclusions. Customers purchasing an optional protection product should always request this information if it is not offered to them by the rental agent.

INSURANCE COMPANIES

Except for loss damage waiver (LDW), which is not insurance but a waiver of your contractual responsibility for damage to the rental vehicle, optional protection products are generally provided through insurance companies specializing in such coverage. In most states, the rental companies are required to identify the insurance carrier providing the coverage in brochures and other collateral material.

PACKAGE PLANS

As if understanding car rental insurance wasn't difficult enough, you may find yourself faced with making decisions about optional plans that combine two or more protection products. In an attempt to achieve some degree of product differentiation, some companies have developed package plans as an alternative to simply offering a list of separate products.

These packages may be structured in a couple of different ways. One way simply combines two or more plans into a broader, more comprehensive option. An example of this is to combine personal accident insurance (PAI) and personal effects coverage (PEC) into a single plan. Sometimes, these package plans must be accepted in their entirety. Other times, the individual components can be purchased separately.

Another tactic used by companies is to combine individual coverage plans in a packaged offering. For example, a company might offer a "deluxe" package that includes LDW, increased liability protection, and PAI. Under this package approach, the products are still available individually. Because it is rare that a renter will need all of the coverage included in a deluxe package, combining coverages in this manner is mainly intended to increase the rental company's sales revenue.

When offered such an all-inclusive package, don't accept it unless you are certain that you need all of the protection provided. If you need some but not all of the protection included in the package, ask if you can purchase only the coverage you need.

When companies offer these deluxe packages, they often use them as a starting point in the sales presentation. For instance, a company might start the process by suggesting its "best" package that combines three of its coverage plans. If the customer refuses, the customer service representative will then recommend the company's "better" package that includes its two most popular plans. If the customer still refuses, the representative will then try offering each plan individually. Companies that use this approach often find that most customers will at least accept one of the individual plans and many will take the "best" or "better" package.

Personal Accident Insurance

One type of optional insurance offered by car rental companies is a plan that provides the renter and passengers with coverage for medical expenses that result from an accident. These plans usually also include an accidental death benefit. This insurance is most commonly called personal accident insurance (PAI).

The following is an overview of a typical PAI plan. The terms of the PAI plans offered by rental companies may vary, so always review the company's brochure or other material before deciding whether to purchase the coverage.

WHAT PAI COVERS

PAI provides renters and occupants of the rental vehicle with coverage for medical expenses that result from accidental injury. It also provides an accidental death benefit for the renter and passengers. There may also be coverage for ambulance expenses.

WHO PAI COVERS

Coverage applies to the renter and passengers in the rental vehicle. Most PAI plans feature an important distinction between the renter and passengers. The named renter is covered both in and out of the vehicle during the entire rental period. All other individuals (including other authorized drivers) are covered only while actually occupying the vehicle.

The renter is covered for accidents that occur in virtually any manner and in any place (subject to policy exclusions and limitations) during the rental period. All other individuals must be in the rental vehicle for coverage to apply.

To illustrate, a renter could slip and fall in the hotel shower and have resultant medical expenses covered as long as the accident occurred during the rental period. If the renter's spouse, children, or other members of the renter's traveling party were injured in a similar manner, there would be no coverage. They would have to be injured while occupying the rental vehicle for coverage to apply.

COVERAGE LIMITS

PAI generally includes a specific limit for each type of coverage included in the plan. The limits for certain coverages are often different for the named renter than for other vehicle occupants.

There is quite a variance among current plans in the accidental death benefit limit. Some companies offer plans that provide renters with a death benefit as low as $10,000 or $15,000, while other plans feature limits ranging up to $175,000. The death benefit for passengers is usually lower than the limit for the named renter, often equal to 10% of the renter's benefit. The higher renter benefit applies only to the named renter. All other individuals occupying the vehicle receive the passenger benefit.

PAI plans often also include an aggregate policy limit specifying the maximum that will be paid per accident. The insurance companies' intent is to cap the maximum potential payout in the event an accident resulted in multiple serious injuries or fatalities.

Renters considering the purchase of PAI might also want to inquire about the death benefit settlement terms. The plans offered by some rental companies do not pay the full policy limit as a lump sum in the event of accidental death and instead pay 10% of the limit each year over a 10-year period. Plans that provide an immediate payment of the accidental death benefit are obviously preferable.

Unlike the different death benefit levels for the renter and passengers, the coverage for medical expenses is usually the same for everyone. Depending on the plan, the coverage limits may vary. Some plans provide medical expense coverage as low as $750 per person, while others include benefits up to $3,500 per person. When a separate ambulance benefit is provided, it is usually in the range of $250 per person.

Some PAI policies also require that treatment occur within a certain amount of time after the accident for PAI benefits to apply.

COST
PAI is offered at an additional charge that applies for each full or partial rental day. The daily charge for PAI can vary by rental company, location, and limit of coverage provided and is usually in the $2.00 to $5.00 range.

EXCLUSIONS
PAI often excludes coverage for losses caused by or resulting from:
- Use of any alcoholic or narcotic substance, unless ordered by a licensed physician
- Intentional or self-inflicted injury or suicide
- Commission of an assault or felony
- Aircraft travel
- Disease, illness, or bacterial infection (unless caused by an accidental injury)
- Declared or undeclared war, riot, or civil insurrection
- Service in the armed forces of any country
- Participation in a race, speed, or endurance contest
- Preexisting injuries or conditions
- Stress fractures, heat stroke, strains, twists, etc., unless caused by an accident
- Engagement in an illegal occupation
- Any violation of a prohibited use as listed on the rental contract

OTHER AVAILABLE INSURANCE
Renters and passengers often have other comparable coverage available through life, medical, or accident insurance policies. As a result, PAI may duplicate their other available coverage. However, many PAI plans will pay

benefits in addition to those received from other sources with the possible exception of mandatory auto no-fault benefits. In those cases, PAI benefits may be paid only on an excess basis.

Rental agents may use the fact that PAI pays for expenses even if they are covered and paid by other insurance as a benefit and selling point. This may be true, but be aware that payments made by the PAI insurer might affect your other coverage. For example, your personal health insurance company might decline paying for expenses that have been paid by your PAI plan.

WHO SHOULD PURCHASE PAI

Because its benefits may be similar to other available insurance coverage, some renters may not need PAI. Who should consider purchasing it?

As a rule, PAI is recommended for customers who:

- Do not have comparable coverage available. It may also be beneficial to renters who are unsure about the extent of their other coverage.
- Want to supplement the coverage provided by their other available insurance. For example, individuals belonging to an HMO may not have coverage for medical services outside of their HMO territory unless the situation is life threatening. Accepting PAI helps fill this type of gap that can occur.
- Want to increase the limits of their other insurance. PAI benefits are payable in addition to other insurance protection available to a covered person.
- Want to offset their responsibility for the deductibles or coinsurance provisions of their other coverage. Renters using their own insurance coverage usually have their claims reduced by a deductible and/or coinsurance amount. PAI can help eliminate any out-of-pocket loss the renter would otherwise suffer.

OTHER RECOMMENDATIONS REGARDING PAI

Applicable state law often regulates the terms and conditions of the PAI policy. Some of these laws mandate certain coverage limits or limit the use of certain exclusions or coverage restrictions. In the event of a claim, you make sure that the benefits provided reflect those to which you are entitled by requesting a copy of the policy for review.

Some rental companies do not offer PAI as a separate product option but combine it with personal effects coverage and offer the two coverages only as a package. If you feel that you need only one part of the combined coverage, you will have to decide between not purchasing the combined offering or paying for a benefit you don't need.

Personal Effects Coverage

Another optional protection plan, commonly referred to as personal effects coverage, or PEC, provides coverage against loss of or damage to your personal property. It is usually offered in the form of an insurance policy underwritten by and provided through an insurance company, although some rental companies may self-insure this exposure.

The following is an overview of a typical PEC plan. Again, the terms of the various plans offered by rental companies vary, so always review the company's brochure or other material before deciding whether to purchase the coverage.

WHAT PEC COVERS

There are some variations among the PEC plans currently being offered. Some plans cover property against loss or damage resulting from any cause unless the cause is specifically excluded. Other plans cover damage that results only when directly caused by specific perils listed in the policy. Some use a stated peril and exclusion approach, which combines the two.

For the plans that cover damage to personal property resulting from any cause except those specifically excluded, PAE usually will not cover loss or damage caused by or arising out of:

- Mysterious disappearance
- Loading or unloading of the vehicle (unless damage is result of a covered peril)
- Use of the rental vehicle for commercial purposes
- Loss or damage resulting from breakage, marring, scratching, dampness, spoilage, discoloration, mold, mildew, rust, frost, rot, mishandling, improper packing, or rough handling
- War or act of war
- Nuclear reaction or radiation
- Custody, care, or control of property by common carriers
- A violation of the terms and conditions of the rental contract

For specific peril plans, coverage is afforded only when damage to property results from:

- Fire, explosion, or lightning
- Collision of the rental vehicle
- Theft from the rental vehicle (but only if the vehicle was locked, the theft was reported to the police, and there was visible evidence of forced entry)

PERSONAL PROPERTY COVERED

PEC is intended to protect only against loss to personal property. The renter or another covered person, as defined in the policy, must be the owner of the property. It usually does not cover business property, property for sale, or other property specifically excluded by the policy. Renters traveling on business should be aware that company-owned property such as laptop computers, samples, etc., may not be covered.

PROPERTY SPECIFICALLY EXCLUDED

Although the categories of property excluded vary somewhat by plan, the property most commonly excluded under PEC policies includes:
- Currency, coins, stamps, tickets, deeds, and documents
- Contact lenses, eye glasses, and prosthetic devices
- Furs, jewelry, and fine arts
- Food, liquor, medication, plants, animals, and other perishable goods
- Audio visual equipment, televisions, video cameras, and camcorders
- Cellular phones, CB radios, tape players, radios, and other sound-reproducing or -receiving equipment
- Motor vehicles including motorcycles and mobile equipment
- Household furniture

This list of exclusions may not be indicative of all PEC plans. Some, for example, do cover items such as cell phones. It is important that you refer to the specific terms and conditions of the plan offered by your rental company.

WHO PEC COVERS

PEC covers personal property owned by the named renter and members of the renter's immediate family while traveling with the renter. Immediate family is usually defined as the renter's spouse and minor children residing in the same household with the renter.

This sometimes presents problems for renters traveling with individuals other than family members. These renters sometimes purchase PEC only to find out after a loss that the personal property of their traveling companions is not covered.

To eliminate this problem, some PEC plans have been modified to include the property of business associates traveling with the renter. Some plans also provide coverage for property of any individual traveling with the renter, including nonrelatives. These plans may require proof that the unrelated person is actually traveling with the renter such as airplane tickets, itineraries, hotel bills, or other similar documentation.

WHEN DOES PEC COVERAGE APPLY?

Coverage applies for all covered losses that occur any time during your rental period. An important distinction is that some plans cover property only while it is contained in the rental vehicle, while others also cover property out of the vehicle during the rental period. The broader plan would provide coverage for property that is stolen from a hotel room.

COVERAGE LIMITS

Most PEC plans include both a per person and a per occurrence limit. The per person limit is the maximum amount that will be paid to any one person regardless of whether it is the renter or a passenger. That limit is typically around $500 to $600. The per occurrence limit is the maximum that the insurance company will pay for any one incident regardless of the number of individuals that suffer a loss. The per occurrence or aggregate limit is usually three times the per person limit (or $1,500 to $1,800).

To illustrate, assume that the renter and three passengers (all covered persons) pick up a rental car at the airport and load their suitcases in the trunk. The renter accepts and pays for a PEC plan that provides limits of $600 per person and $1,800 per occurrence. The vehicle is involved in an accident, and their property in the trunk is damaged. Each individual sustains a loss in the amount of $500. Even though the amount of each loss is within the $600 per person limit, the total would exceed the $1,800 aggregate limit. As a result, the most that would be paid would be $1,800, or $450 per person.

There is another coverage limitation often found in PEC plans. These plans often state that in the event that more than one loss occurs during the rental period, the limit available for each succeeding claim will be reduced by amount paid for prior claims. In other words, both the individual and aggregate limits for the plan apply to the rental period, not each separate loss that might occur during the rental period.

WHAT DOES PEC COST?

PEC is offered at an additional charge that applies for each full or partial rental day. The daily cost of PEC varies by rental company, location, and limit of coverage provided and is typically in the $1.00 to $3.00 range.

OTHER AVAILABLE INSURANCE

Renters and passengers often have other comparable coverage available through homeowner's or personal property policies. PEC may duplicate this other available coverage. PEC plans will pay benefits in addition to those received from other sources, but any PEC claim settlement may affect a claim filed under your other policies.

Even though the PEC policy agrees to pay in addition to any other available coverage, there may be an other insurance provision in your homeowner's policy that prevents you from collecting twice. The effect of such a provision may be that your homeowner's policy will provide coverage only in excess of any benefits available under the PEC plan.

WHO SHOULD PURCHASE PERSONAL EFFECTS COVERAGE

In general, the purchase of PEC should be considered by renters who:
- Do not have, or are unsure whether they have, comparable coverage available under their personal policies.
- Want to supplement the coverage provided by their other available insurance. In effect, they are purchasing deductible insurance because the relatively low PEC limit serves as an offset to the deductible amount that will be charged if a claim is presented under their homeowner's policy.
- Want to increase the limits of their available insurance. PEC benefits are payable in addition to any other insurance protection that may be available to a covered person. So it might be possible to collect for damaged property under both the PEC plan and your homeowner's insurance policy (subject to any other insurance provision as discussed above).

Emergency Sickness Protection

Another optional protection plan, although less commonly offered, is called emergency sickness protection (ESP). It provides coverage for medical expenses resulting from a covered sickness to renters who reside outside of the United States while they are traveling in the United States.

The following is an overview of a typical ESP plan. As with other optional plans, the terms may vary, so always review the company's brochure or other material before deciding whether to purchase the coverage.

WHAT ESP COVERS

ESP provides coverage for reasonable, customary, and necessary medical care expenses incurred as a result of a covered sickness. The expenses typically covered include:

- Medical or surgical treatment
- Hospital services
- Local ambulance
- X-rays
- Laboratory fees
- Visits to a physician's office

ESP applies when a covered person incurs medical expenses as a result of a covered sickness that manifests itself during the period beginning with the execution of the rental agreement and ending when the rental agreement is terminated or within 30 days, whichever is less.

WHO ESP COVERS

ESP is intended for travelers visiting the United States who possess a non-U.S. passport at the time of rental. (Citizens of Canada may present other proof of residency in lieu of a passport.) No benefits will be paid to individuals who possess a valid U.S. passport or are citizens of the United States.

ESP provides coverage for:

- The renter
- Individuals traveling with the renter

All individuals claiming benefits under the ESP policy must provide written proof that they were members of the renter's traveling party. Written documentation such as passports, travel agent itineraries, and manifests, etc., may be used to support the claim.

COVERAGE LIMITS

ESP usually provides coverage up to $10,000 per covered person with a $100 deductible per person.

COST

ESP is available for an additional daily charge shown on the rental agreement and is payable for each full or partial rental day. The daily rate is usually around $4.00.

Exclusions

The ESP generally contains a number of exclusions including:

- Losses resulting from any sickness or complication arising from any sickness for which symptoms began or treatment was received during the 12 months prior to the beginning of the rental period
- Expenses incurred in countries other than the United States
- Expenses for eyeglasses, contact lenses, or hearing aids
- Losses incurred while participating in a professional, club, intercollegiate, or interscholastic sports or while racing
- Losses resulting from an accident
- Losses resulting from cardiovascular disease, cancers, tumors, tuberculosis, organ transplant, congenital conditions, deviated septum, cosmetic surgery, dental care, sexually transmitted diseases, birth control, fertility/infertility treatment, pregnancy, miscarriage, abortion, and emotional or mental disorders of any kind
- Losses incurred while traveling against the advice of a physician or while traveling for the purpose of receiving medical treatment

WHO SHOULD PURCHASE ESP

Individuals residing outside of the United States typically have little or no medical insurance available to them while visiting the United States. They may have medical coverage in their home country, but that coverage may not apply while traveling out of their country.

As a result, these travelers usually end up personally responsible for medical expenses incurred in the United States. By purchasing ESP, they are protected against the cost of medical expenses resulting from any sickness that occurs. When these foreign travelers purchase ESP in tandem with PAI, they have coverage for their medical expenses that result from either a sickness or an accident.

Mexico Tourist Insurance

Most rental contracts prohibit customers from taking their vehicles rented in the United States across the border into Mexico. If a renter does happen to enter Mexico, the rental company may consider the act to be a violation of the terms of the contract. If an accident should occur while the vehicle is in Mexico, all protection that the company would otherwise provide as well as any limitation of the renter's responsibility for vehicle damage could be voided.

The main reason that rental companies don't allow renters to drive into Mexico revolves around the laws of Mexico and their effect on both the renter and the rental company.

Under Mexican law, an auto accident can be a criminal offense. Unlike the U.S. legal system that assumes an individual is innocent until proven guilty, Mexican auto law assumes guilt until innocence is proved. If you have an accident in Mexico, you could be detained until the authorities complete their accident investigation and determine which party was responsible. During the investigation, your rental vehicle may be impounded.

After the authorities establish responsibility for the accident, the negligent driver may be expected to pay for the full amount of any resultant damages. Until damages are paid, the at-fault driver could remain jailed.

One way to avoid this situation is to guarantee restitution to the parties suffering the damage by having valid insurance in place. But don't rely on your personal auto policy to satisfy this requirement because most don't provide coverage in Mexico. Furthermore, you must not only have insurance that covers you in Mexico, but the Mexican authorities must also recognize that insurance as valid.

This presents a problem for renters who want or need to rent in the United States and travel across the border. With the recent growth of border businesses and plants inside Mexico, the need has been steadily increasing. It is also common for travelers to locations in proximity of the border, such as San Diego or Tucson, to want to spend a day in Mexico as part of their trip.

The solution used by some rental companies is to offer an optional insurance product to these renters. The coverage is provided by a licensed Mexican insurer and may be called Mexico tourist insurance, Mexican visitors insurance, or some similar name. These plans are recognized by Mexican authorities as a guarantee of payment for damages and can enable your quick release in the event you are detained for an accident investigation.

This optional insurance is usually sold for between $15 to $20 per day and typically provides the following coverage:

- Third-party bodily injury and property damage liability protection (often with a combined single limit of $100,000).
- Physical damage coverage for the rental vehicle. Physical damage is usually defined to include damage resulting from collision or vehicle upset. Glass breakage is often included under physical damage coverage. This coverage is usually sold with a specific limit (i.e., $25,000) corresponding to the approximate value of the vehicle. It sometimes also features a deductible of several hundred dollars that remains the renter's responsibility.
- Coverage for other damage to the rental vehicle resulting from theft, fire, and acts of God. Theft coverage applies only if the entire vehicle is stolen. Theft of parts or accessories is usually not covered and remains the responsibility of the renter. There is usually a specified limit and deductible included.
- Medical expenses incurred by the driver or passengers in the rental vehicle are sometimes provided but only when injuries result from specified causes such as collision or upset.

This coverage often includes policy exclusions relating to unauthorized drivers, use of alcohol or drugs, and others similar to the list of prohibited uses found in the rental company's contract. Coverage applies only while the vehicle is operated in Mexico. Once the vehicle crosses the border back into the United States, it is no longer valid. If you purchase a Mexico tourist policy, you should review its terms before leaving the rental location.

In addition to a copy of the policy, renters who purchase this coverage are provided with a list of authorized adjusters or a claim reporting telephone number. It is extremely important to safeguard this information and keep it with you at all times. If you are involved in an accident, you must report the claim either to the nearest adjuster or the claim service number as soon as possible.

It is in your best interest to get an adjuster involved immediately. Not only does it fulfill your accident reporting requirement under the policy, but also the adjuster is often needed to confirm to the law enforcement authorities that you do have valid liability insurance. Until you can prove that you have insurance, you may be subject to incarceration.

Some Mexican insurers include a legal service feature with their policy that provides additional benefits for attorney's fees, fines, and bail bonds. With the potential difficulties you might face after an accident, it could be a valuable service.

Because Mexico tourist insurance applies when a vehicle is rented in the United States and driven into Mexico, it is generally available only at rental locations within reasonable driving distance of the border. But not all rental companies offer this coverage. If you need to rent a car in the United States and drive across the border into Mexico, you should contact rental companies in advance to determine which ones will allow their vehicles into Mexico and offer the necessary insurance.

If you decide that you want to rent a car in the United States and drive across the border into Mexico, there are several other important points you need to keep in mind:

- If you are involved in a serious accident that results in bodily injury or death, even a valid Mexican insurance policy might not keep you from being detained until the authorities complete their investigation.
- Mexico does not establish a minimum liability limit requirement, so the amount of coverage you need will be determined by the amount of damages that result from an accident. So if the rental company offers several limit options, its wise to purchase the maximum limit offered.
- You will see numerous insurance agencies advertising Mexican insurance on the U.S. side of the border. Be aware that purchasing such coverage may not satisfy the rental company, and should you drive into Mexico, the rental company will still consider that a violation of the terms of its rental contract. If you need to purchase Mexican insurance, you should obtain it from the rental company.

Some rental companies allow you to drive into Mexico as long as you remain within a specified limited distance from the border. If your destination in Mexico is within that distance, you may not need this additional coverage. However, you should then obtain from the rental company some proof of insurance that will be accepted in Mexico. You should also review the terms of the rental contract carefully to make sure that you fully understand its restrictions in regards to driving in Mexico.

chapter fifteen

Corporate Agreements

Like many industries, car rental companies often offer discounted prices and additional benefits to high-volume customers. If your business is willing to commit most of its car rental activity to one company, you should get a better deal than if you spread the business around to multiple companies.

How good a deal you get depends largely on how much business volume you're willing to deliver. Rental companies generally have multiple tiers of benefits that they provide customers depending on the size of the account. A company that commits to $25,000 of rental business is going to get some additional benefits but obviously not to the same degree as a company that provides $5 million worth of business.

A rental company's proposal to a prospective corporate customer is based on that customer's commitment to provide a certain level of rental volume. This initial proposal is simply a starting point from which everything is negotiable. If a particular benefit is important to you but the rental company doesn't offer it, ask that it be included in your program. Rental companies need corporate volume to be profitable and are not going to lose a sizable account by being rigid, especially if a requested benefit results in little additional cost to the rental company.

ESTABLISHING A CORPORATE ACCOUNT

All major car rental companies offer corporate account programs. Although all programs require a minimum volume commitment to qualify, that commitment may be as low as $5,000 annually.

Your first step in establishing a corporate account is to contact a number of rental companies to express your interest. How many you choose to contact depends on your available time and resources. Getting recommendations from business contacts with similar travel needs is often a good starting point.

Call each company's toll-free telephone number and ask to be put in contact with a corporate sales representative. Or you can visit the company's Web site to provide some preliminary information about your company and its rental needs.

In addition to some basic contact information, you will be asked to provide the following:

- The type of business you're in
- The number of employee travelers in your company
- Your estimated number of rentals each month
- Your estimated annual car rental expenditure
- The primary cities or geographic regions where you rent
- The car rental company you currently use

The company's sales representative will use this information to develop a proposal.

BASIC CORPORATE ACCOUNT BENEFITS

After you receive a proposal, compare it to others you've received in terms of the benefits most important to you. You are then ready to start the negotiation process. If your total rental expenditure is relatively low, you shouldn't expect to get everything you ask for, regardless of how skillful a negotiator you may be. If your annual expenditure is several hundred thousand dollars, you hold a much stronger hand.

But regardless of your rental volume, there is no reason why you shouldn't be able to negotiate an agreement more beneficial to your company once you understand the process and what types of benefits are available.

There are two principal groups of corporate account benefits. The first includes those usually described in the rental company brochures and sales material. The second group includes those benefits that the rental companies may not even mention unless you ask for them.

The benefits most commonly offered to corporate accounts include:

Express rental pickup and return
Acknowledging that time is of the essence with business travelers, most

corporate account programs include express service that allows the renter to avoid the rental counter when picking up and returning vehicles. Rental companies that usually charge customers an annual fee to enroll in express service programs may waive that fee for corporate accounts.

Enrollment in rental company loyalty programs

Some rental companies have customer loyalty programs that allow renters to accumulate credits based on the number of times they rent. The credits are then redeemed for free rental days or prizes such as vacations, spa treatments, golf clubs, or other merchandise. Employees traveling under a corporate account program are often automatically enrolled in these loyalty programs.

Frequent flier and hotel programs

Some rental companies also have programs in which renters can earn frequent flier miles or hotel points each time they rent. Corporate account travelers can also be automatically enrolled in these programs.

Special business rates

Rates undoubtedly receive the most attention from prospective corporate accounts. The tendency is to focus on the base daily rate alone, often at the expense of other items that can be just as, if not more, important.

Consider this example. Your rental volume is relatively large, with approximately 10,000 annual rental days. You are successful in negotiating a daily rate that is $2 less than the rate initially offered by the rental company. However, because of the low daily rate, the rental company is reluctant to include some other benefits, such as a full waiver of your responsibility for vehicle damage.

Your annual savings realized from the lower rate is $20,000. But focusing solely on rate and not receiving a full damage waiver could erase that savings with only one accident. This is not to say that negotiating a low rate isn't a good idea. But you shouldn't focus solely on rates at the expense of other potential benefits. This is a common mistake for many companies.

Whatever daily rate is eventually agreed upon, it will be locked in under your agreement for its full term (usually one year). This helps companies in budgeting for their travel expenses and also allows the rental company to more accurately project future revenue.

Corporate accounts sometimes become upset upon discovering that their rental company is offering a special promotional rate to the general public that is lower than their contracted corporate agreement rate. Some accounts believe that their negotiated rate should always be better than they could obtain in the absence of the corporate agreement.

But one of the principal benefits of a corporate agreement rate is that rates are locked in for a specified period. If rates rise, the account is protected for the duration of the agreement period. With that security comes the chance that a special promotional rate (which may last a limited time or be confined to specific locations) might be lower.

When corporate customers find a promotional rate that is lower than their agreement rate, they sometimes decide to use the promotional rate to take advantage of the savings. Use caution in doing so because under some corporate programs, benefits may be voided if the contracted daily rate is not used. If one of the account benefits is liability protection or a waiver of vehicle damage responsibility and an accident occurs, those benefits might be refused.

Some rental companies now offer the option of accepting a rate lower than their corporate rate without losing any corporate account benefits. This provides the customer with the best of both worlds: a guaranteed rate plus the opportunity to take advantage of any lower rate, if available.

Corporate agreements rarely include a single negotiated daily rate. Instead, a schedule of rates based on different vehicle classifications is used. The corporate customer may then develop an internal policy in regards of what types of vehicles may be rented.

Vehicle selection and availability
Rental companies will sometimes guarantee that the corporate account's vehicle type and equipment preference will be available for all rentals.

Unlimited mileage
Most corporate account programs provide unlimited mileage for all business rentals.

Free rental days
Corporate accounts are sometimes awarded credits that can be accumulated and used toward free rental days each time they rent. This type of benefit can help reduce an account's total rental expenditure.

Underage driver charge

Many rental companies will not rent to anyone under the age of 25. Those that will do so may add an underage driver surcharge. Under most corporate account programs, the underage driver restriction is eliminated (or at least lowered) without additional charge. The reasoning is that young business renters should drive more responsibly.

Also, refusing to rent to an employee under 25 could be detrimental to the corporate account. Young employees required to travel would have a difficult time performing their jobs if they were not allowed to rent cars.

Select city surcharges

Because of the fixed daily rate of a corporate agreement, rental companies sometimes add surcharges to rentals in certain cities where their standard rates are higher than average. The surcharge is intended to realize a higher rate in those areas that warrant one (because of either accident or operating costs).

It is sometimes possible to negotiate a lower surcharge (or eliminate it altogether) when arranging a corporate agreement. It is especially in the best interest of an account to do so when a significant portion of its rentals will occur in surcharged areas.

Other surcharges

Rental companies sometimes charge additional fees in certain rental situations. They may include such charges as additional driver and one-way drop fees. There may also be extra fees charged for short-term (i.e., one-day) rentals that occur on certain days of the week when business is heaviest. It is sometimes possible to get the rental company to reduce or waive these fees.

Billing plans

Corporate accounts are generally provided with a centralized billing option that allows employees to charge their rentals to the company's account. The account's employees may be provided with personalized charge cards to facilitate the centralized billing.

In addition to a consolidated billing statement, the corporate account may also receive detailed reports showing the rental activity for each individual employee. Depending on the capabilities of the rental company and the size of the account, various customized billing and management reporting options may be offered.

Dedicated customer service

For certain accounts, rental companies may provide dedicated reservation and customer service assistance. That assistance may include toll-free telephone numbers, access to a corporate account–only Web site, and a dedicated representative.

Emergency road service

Rental companies generally provide customers with an emergency road service telephone number call in the event of an accident or mechanical breakdown. Corporate accounts receive the same benefit, although sometimes at a slightly higher service level.

Valet service

Executives of very large corporate accounts are sometimes picked up and dropped off at their airport terminal by a rental company employee.

Leisure rates

Although the benefits of a corporate agreement are intended for business use rentals, rental companies sometimes provide employees of certain accounts with discounted rates when they rent for nonbusiness purposes. These rates provide employees with incentive to use the same car rental company for all rental needs, including vacations.

Benefits provided to employees renting for nonbusiness purposes may be limited to the discounted rate. In most cases, any additional benefits a corporate account receives are not extended to employees for their personal rentals.

Discounted parking

A few car rental companies also own and operate airport parking lots that are available to the public. They may provide corporate accounts with discounted parking rates for employees who need to leave their personal car at the airport when traveling.

OTHER CORPORATE ACCOUNT BENEFITS

In addition to the above benefits, corporate accounts may obtain additional benefits as part of their agreement. The availability of these benefits may not be advertised in the sales material used by rental companies and might not be even mentioned unless raised as issues by the account.

Following are descriptions of some of these benefits. An account's success in getting any of these benefits included in its agreement is largely dependent on the size of the account's rental volume commitment and the policies of the rental company.

Vehicle damage waiver

Renters assume full financial responsibility for all damage to the rental car. To avoid or limit this responsibility, you must purchase the rental company's loss damage waiver (LDW). But as a corporate account customer, there is another way for you to protect yourself. Many corporate customers negotiate a waiver of their vehicle damage responsibility as part of their agreement.

Rental companies are less inclined to offer full damage waivers than they were in the past. They are more likely to offer partial waivers to corporate accounts that meet certain volume commitments. Partial waivers limit the account's financial responsibility to a stated amount, typically $2,000 or $3,000, with responsibility for all damage exceeding the amount stated in the agreement waived.

By holding the account responsible for all damage up to a certain amount, the rental company meets two objectives. First, it maintains the corporate account's damage responsibility for many of the claims that occur. Also, it encourages the account's employees to exercise more care in operating and protecting the vehicle.

This limited damage responsibility benefits the corporate account by providing protection against large losses. It basically serves as a type of deductible for the account.

The limit of the corporate account's damage responsibility is usually dependant on the size of its rental volume commitment. There are usually three possible options available when determining damage responsibility:

- Corporate account has full responsibility for vehicle damage
- Corporate account has limited responsibility (i.e., $2,000, $3,000, etc.)
- Corporate account has no responsibility for vehicle damage

When the agreement comes up for renewal, the rental company may decide to increase the limit or eliminate the partial waiver altogether if the account has not met its rental volume commitment or if its accident experience is worse than expected.

Liability protection

Liability protection provided by the rental company is often secondary to any other coverage available to the renter. When the rental company does provide primary protection, it is usually limited to the applicable state financial responsibility limit.

Corporate accounts sometimes receive enhanced liability protection as a benefit. That enhanced protection typically has two components:

- The rental company always provides the corporate account with primary rather than secondary liability protection
- The limit of liability protection is higher than the required state limit

The liability protection provided to a corporate account may include one or both of these components. For example, an account may be given primary protection as a benefit but with the limits of liability protection remaining at the state limit. In other cases, the account might receive both primary protection and increased limits.

When increased liability limits are provided, they are often in the amount of 100/300/25. Some large accounts may receive higher limits, and it is not unusual for multimillion-dollar accounts to receive limits of $1 million (CSL).

Global protection

The standard corporate agreement used by rental companies is often limited to U.S. rentals, especially for damage waivers and liability protection. Corporate accounts renting on a worldwide basis can sometimes get these benefits extended globally.

Licensee locations

Some rental companies operate with a combination of company-owned and franchised or licensee locations. Corporate accounts may want to ensure that all provisions of the agreement apply to all locations, not just the ones that are owned and operated by the parent rental company.

Modified use restrictions

Although rental companies don't generally like to do this, it is possible to modify the list of use restrictions that are found in the standard rental contract.

Many of the use restrictions will remain nonnegotiable. Rental companies seldom want to waive their right to void benefits in the event of what they consider unacceptable operation of the vehicle. For example, a rental company is probably not going to remove the use restriction about driving while intoxicated at your request.

But there are some use restrictions that might be modified. For example, a common use restriction states that the vehicle can be operated only on a paved or regularly maintained road. If your employees have to drive down a poorly maintained gravel road to get to one of your locations, you should address the problem with the rental company and try to get that restriction removed or amended.

Before executing a corporate agreement, ask the rental company for its list of use restrictions to determine whether any could pose a problem for your company or its employees.

Refueling options

The most economical refueling option offered by rental companies requires the renter to fill the gas tank immediately before returning the vehicle. This, of course, is sometimes inconvenient for business travelers who are often on tight schedules. If a renter fails to fill the gas tank before returning the vehicle, the rental company will charge for the amount of gas needed to fill the tank at an inflated price.

Corporate customers are often best served to request the inclusion of an agreement provision that allows the rental company to charge only for the amount of gas needed at a predetermined rate, or at the current market rate, without any markup or surcharge.

Extension of corporate agreement to nonemployees

Corporate accounts sometimes utilize independent contractors and consultants in their business activities. If these contractors and consultants are required to travel on behalf of the corporate account, it may be beneficial to amend the corporate agreement to include these individuals as authorized renters.

Corporate accounts usually pay the travel expenses of these individuals, so it makes sense for them to want to be able to take advantage of the favorable terms of the agreement. But because these contractors and consultants are technically not employees, it is necessary to modify the terms of the corporate agreement to have them included.

Service standards

Corporate accounts sometimes request the inclusion of specific service standards in their agreement. These standards may include such criteria as the timeliness of the pickup and return process, the availability of requested vehicle types, the cleanliness of vehicles, the accuracy of billing statements, and other metrics.

CORPORATE AGREEMENT FORM

Rental companies require corporate accounts to execute a formal corporate agreement form that describes the duties and responsibilities of both parties. These agreements typically require that at least some of the following criteria must be met in order for the stated benefits to apply:

- The vehicle must be rented to an authorized employee of the corporate account
- The employee must possess a valid driver's license
- The employee must be at least 21 years of age
- The rental must be in the furtherance of the account's business
- The vehicle type rented must be as listed in the agreement
- The rental rate used must be as listed in the agreement
- There is no violation of a use restriction listed on the rental contract

The agreement should describe all of the applicable provisions and benefits as agreed upon with the rental company. It should also include a provision stating that its contents should supersede those contained in the rental contract in the event of a conflict. Without this provision, ambiguities could result. Prospective corporate accounts should always have their legal counsel approve the agreement prior to execution.

CORPORATE AGREEMENTS WITH MORE THAN ONE COMPANY

Companies sometimes enter into corporate agreements with multiple rental companies. It is common to select both a primary and a secondary rental supplier. This can be beneficial in the event that one of the companies doesn't service (or service well) some areas. It also provides employees with some flexibility in arranging their travel.

chapter sixteen

Renting Outside the United States

When travel takes you out of the United States and you need to rent a car, some of what has already been discussed goes right out the window. The confusion and uncertainty surrounding the rental transaction can become even more pronounced in other parts of the world. You might even get a few strange looks simply by asking for directions to the car rental location; in many places, the correct terminology is not "car rental" but "car hire."

Although some of the challenges you'll face are as simple as differences in terminology, others are more critical and can significantly affect your comfort, safety, and financial security. A discussion of some of the more important issues you might encounter when renting outside of the United States follows.

CAR RENTAL (CAR HIRE) COMPANIES

When renting a car outside of the United States, you'll see some familiar names as well as some that are not so familiar. Generally speaking, the companies can be classified as follows:

Global companies

The major companies found in the United States such as Hertz, Avis, National, and Budget also maintain a global presence. Renting from one of these companies is as easy as calling the same toll-free reservation number that you would to rent a car in this country.

There are some advantages to sticking with a familiar car rental company. When you arrive at your destination, the global companies are more likely to have rental agents who can speak English, at least in the major cities and tourist destinations. If you experience a problem and wish to make a formal complaint, it is also easier to do so with a company that has its corporate offices in the United States.

But while you may feel more secure renting from a U.S.-based company, be aware that some of their overseas operations are independent franchises, so the quality of service may vary by location.

Car hire brokers and wholesalers

There are also rental brokers and wholesalers whose names might not be quite as familiar to you such as Auto Europe, Holiday Autos, Europe by Car, and Kemwel. These companies operate as consolidators that negotiate volume discounts from major and local car rental companies and often pass along sizeable savings to customers.

For the most part, whether you rent a car directly from the company or go through a broker will not affect the level of service you receive. You may find some large variances among rates, so it pays to do some shopping before selecting a company. You should make your reservation before leaving the United States so you don't have to start shopping for a good deal after arriving at your destination.

VEHICLES

There are significant differences among vehicles available for rent outside of the United States.

Some of those differences include the following:
- You might be unfamiliar with some of the vehicles available for rent and might get confused when asked to make a selection among makes and models such as the Opel Corsa, Renault Clio, and Volkswagen Polo.
- Most vehicles are appreciably smaller than their U.S. counterparts, with the difference most noticeable at the low end of the rate scale.

Be very careful about reserving the least expensive car available. The cheapest cars often have less interior room than the average American subcompact car and could be very uncomfortable if you're accustomed to a larger vehicle.

- Automatic transmissions are not considered to be standard equipment in many countries. Unless you're comfortable operating a manual transmission, request a car with an automatic when making your reservation. Cars equipped with automatic transmissions can be harder to find and are often more expensive.
- If you are able to operate a manual transmission, you can save money, not only on the rental rate but also in gasoline because it is more economical.
- Another feature that is not always standard is air conditioning. If it is important to you, be sure to request it when you make your reservation. It is sometimes available only with larger car classes and can also add to your total rental cost.
- If you rent in a country where you drive on the left, remember that the steering wheel will be on the opposite side of the car. You may want to reconsider your choice of a manual transmission unless you are adept at shifting with your left hand because the gearshift lever will also be on the opposite side.
- Rental vehicles may also have other peculiarities not common to cars sold in this country. You should thoroughly familiarize yourself with the position of the accelerator and brake pedals, headlight and windshield wiper controls, and other features before driving.
- Vehicle gauges often use the metric system (100 kilometers equals approximately 60 miles).

SELECTING THE RIGHT CAR

It is difficult to obtain the right car when the list of makes and models from which you have to choose is a mystery to you. To choose a car that meets your needs, explain your situation when making your reservation. The car rental agent must have full knowledge of certain details in order to provide you with the vehicle best suited to those needs.

When making your reservation, provide the rental agent with the following information:

- The number of passengers in your traveling party
- The amount of luggage you'll be transporting in the vehicle
- The number of days and amount of miles you plan to drive

Armed with this information, the rental company's reservation representative should be able to recommend a vehicle that suits your needs. But before agreeing to that vehicle, you should first ask some questions of your own such as:

- The size of the passenger areas and trunk (in cubic feet)
- The number of seat belts or restraint systems in the vehicle
- The size of the engine
- The vehicle's average miles per gallon of fuel

Use this information to make some reasonable comparisons between the recommended vehicle and the dimensions of your own car or one with which you are familiar. This will require little homework on your part but could be well worth the effort.

RATES

Rental companies outside the United States may offer either a flat daily rate or an inclusive rate. The flat daily rate is similar to the pricing structure found in the United States. The inclusive rate usually includes at least some taxes and damage waivers.

Rates are generally based on a 24-hour clock and usually include a grace period of an hour. However, upon the expiration of the grace period, renters are sometimes charged for a full additional day rather than a prorated amount.

TAXES

Rentals in Europe are subject to a value added tax (VAT) that can amount to up to 25% of your rental cost. In some countries, airport surcharges and road use taxes are also extra and can substantially increase your rental bill.

You should always inquire whether taxes are included in the rate you are quoted. If not, ask for the total amount of the taxes that will be added. Expecting a rate to be inclusive of taxes and later discovering that it is not can be an unpleasant surprise.

RENTAL REQUIREMENTS

As in the United States, rental companies use various criteria to qualify potential customers before agreeing to rent a car to them. These criteria typically focus on age, driver's license, and method of payment requirements.

Age

Minimum age requirements vary by country, but the general rule is that drivers must be at least 21 years of age. If you are under 30 years of age, ask about this requirement before showing up to get your car and finding that you don't qualify.

U.S. residents are often surprised to find that some countries also impose a maximum age requirement. The maximum age varies by country but generally ranges between 65 and 80 years of age. If you are 65 or older and plan to rent a car, ask about any maximum age restriction when making your reservation.

Driver's license requirements

In many countries, you will need to present your driver's license issued by your state of residence. Some companies require your U.S. license to be valid for at least one year.

You may also consider obtaining an international driving permit (IDP). Because some countries will not recognize a U.S. driver's license, it is recommended that you travel with both documents. The IDP is generally not acceptable alone, but because it translates the information on your U.S. license into 11 languages, it is widely recognized by foreign authorities and is beneficial to have. IDPs can be obtained at local American Automobile Association offices.

Method of payment

Many car rentals are prepaid when part of a travel or vacation package. Some customers prefer prepayment in U.S. dollars instead of having to later pay for the rental with local currency. Customers that have prepaid simply provide a voucher at the time of rental.

But even when a voucher is used, the renter will still need to present a valid credit card in his or her own name. A renter cannot use someone else's card, and debit cards may not be accepted as a means of qualifying for rental. Cash deposits are rarely accepted, but you can use cash to pay for your rental when returning the car.

A credit card must be presented to guarantee payment of charges not included with the voucher such as refueling options. Rental companies often hold a reserve amount on the credit card as a deposit that will be charged in the event the vehicle is damaged. Unlike in the United States, rental companies often expect immediate payment for vehicle damage unless a damage waiver is purchased.

The lowest rental rates often require a minimum length of rental. If you rent a car for a certain number of days and decide to return it early, you may be charged a higher rate.

Additional drivers

As in the United States, all additional drivers must meet the rental company's age and driver's license requirements. There is often a fee charged for each additional driver.

INSURANCE AND OPTIONAL PROTECTION

Insurance-related issues can be quite complex, even more so than in the United States. Renters are somewhat at the mercy of the car rental operators, and it is more difficult (and risky) to decline the optional protection that is offered.

The last problem you want when renting in another country is to learn that you have inadequate protection after a loss occurs. Insurance is not where you should try to cut corners to save a few dollars. In some countries, lacking adequate insurance can jeopardize your freedom in addition to denting your wallet. No one wants to spend time in a foreign jail while trying to sort out how to pay for accident claims.

Although it is impossible to provide a precise description of the coverage available because of the many differences that exist, the following are some general guidelines:

Liability protection

Liability coverage for third-party bodily injury and property damage claims is usually the responsibility of the rental company, with the cost of that protection included in the basic rental rate. The extent of coverage could vary greatly, so you should always ask about what type of coverage is provided as well as any exclusions and limitations.

As a rule, your U.S. personal auto policy will not cover you when renting in most other countries (other than Canada). Your business auto coverage may or may not provide any protection. In many cases, the extent of your protection will be limited to that provided by the rental company.

Vehicle damage

As in the United States, the rental contract holds the renter responsible for all loss of or damage to the rental vehicle regardless of fault. In addition to direct vehicle damage, the renter is also responsible for the company's loss of use and other administrative fees.

Some rental companies will refuse to rent to you unless they are certain that you will be able to pay for any damage to the rental car. You may be required to meet one of the following conditions before you will be given a car:

- Proof that you have adequate insurance. Any policy you provide must prove not only that you have insurance but also that your coverage will apply to the rental car in the country it is being rented.
- Purchase of the company's collision damage waiver (CDW).
- A cash or credit card deposit sufficient to cover damage to the vehicle. If you return the vehicle without damage, the deposit will be refunded. If damage does occur, the deposit will be used to pay for it.

Many renters choose to accept the company's damage waiver. The waivers offered in many countries can be quite different from those offered in the United States. They are usually referred to as collision damage waivers and waive the renter's responsibility for damage resulting from most, but not all, causes.

For example, the waivers do not cover the full amount of damage resulting from the theft of the vehicle. If your rental car is stolen, you will be charged several hundred dollars even if you accepted the company's CDW. You can, however, fully protect yourself against theft by purchasing a separate theft waiver (which may be mandatory in some countries with high theft rates).

Also, many CDWs include a deductible amount that can range up to $500 for which you will still be responsible. This can come as quite a surprise to renters who thought that they were fully protected against responsibility for vehicle damage by purchasing a CDW.

In some places, you can purchase a waiver of your CDW deductible, thus eliminating your responsibility completely. For many travelers, having to purchase two or three separate damage waivers in order to fully waive contractual responsibility for vehicle damage can seem very confusing.

Some credit cards extend coverage for damage to a rental car on a worldwide basis. However, certain countries are excluded from coverage, and other restrictions may also apply. If you intend to rely upon the protection provided by your credit card, contact your card company prior to traveling to confirm that you will have coverage.

Even if you are certain that your credit card does provide coverage for vehicle damage, processing your claim can become a nightmare. Imagine having an accident and being required to pay for the damage because you didn't purchase the company's CDW. You file a claim with your credit card company, but after returning to the United States, you are informed that additional documentation, such a police report or repair bills, will be needed.

You now find yourself trying to obtain this information from a rental operator in another country. In dealing with communication problems and time differences, you begin to wonder whether you'll ever get your money back. If you don't have other coverage or don't want to take the chance of facing this type of scenario, you should probably consider accepting the company's damage waiver. But in doing so, make sure that you fully understand the extent of coverage as well as any exclusions and limitations.

Personal accident insurance

Many rental companies also offer an optional personal accident insurance (PAI) option that covers medical bills resulting from an accident. These plans are similar to the PAI plans offered in the United States. If you have other medical insurance that will apply in the country where you are traveling, you may not need this extra protection.

OTHER IMPORTANT DIFFERENCES

In addition to those discussed above, you'll find some other important differences when renting outside the United States:

- Travelers should not expect the same 24-hour service that they are used to in the United States. At many foreign locations, rental offices have restricted hours of operation. You may find them closed during evening hours, on weekends, and during meal times. Ask about a location's hours of operation when making your reservation so you don't show up to claim your vehicle only to find the facility closed.
- The rental contract might not be written in English. If that is the case, ask whether they have an English version or at least a translation of its most important provisions. If further help is needed, determine whether there is an English-speaking representative available to translate the contract and help answer any questions you might have.

- The rental contract may contain restrictions on driving across country borders, especially in Europe. These restrictions apply most often to luxury vehicles. If you plan on traveling from one country to another on your trip, be sure to ask whether it is allowed. In some cases, you might be allowed to cross the border into another country, but you might be required to pay an additional insurance charge.
- Expect gasoline to be more expensive than in the United States. Some vehicles use diesel fuel instead of gasoline. Diesel-powered vehicles are often more expensive to rent, but the diesel fuel is much cheaper than gasoline. Fuel is usually sold by the liter (3.78 liters equals 1 gallon). The terms used for "gasoline" and "diesel fuel" sometimes differ by country, so be sure you understand the difference. Putting the wrong type of fuel in your vehicle could result in an expensive repair bill.
- Each company has its own peculiarities. For example, if you wear glasses, some countries require you to carry a spare pair when you drive. Failure to do so could result in a citation. There could be similar customs everywhere you travel, and it is your responsibility to be aware of them. Consider contacting the tourism office of each country you plan to visit and ask about its motor vehicle laws.

ALTERNATIVES TO RENTING

In addition to the standard method of renting a car at a daily rate, there are some alternatives available to travelers who need motor vehicle transportation.

Chauffeured vehicles

Some companies offer an additional option typically not found in the United States: travelers can hire a car accompanied by a driver. These chauffeured rentals can usually be hired for half (four hours) or full (eight hours) days.

Hiring a vehicle with a driver can provide an added sense of security, but it is not cheap. An eight-hour hire with driver can cost more than double the full day rate for the rental car alone. But it still be should considered as a possible option especially in unfamiliar countries or in areas where travelers might not feel totally safe on their own.

Buy-back option

This option is available to travelers in Europe who need a car for more than 17 days. Under this plan, the traveler actually buys the car and then sells it back at the end of the trip. Both the purchase and selling price are predetermined and guaranteed.

By using this type of plan (which has many characteristics of a lease), the traveler avoids many of the value added taxes, airport surcharges, and road use taxes that can drive up the total cost of a standard rental. Insurance protection (without deductibles) and other benefits are often included in buy-back plans.

This option can be particularly attractive to younger travelers because the standard minimum age requirement is often lower. An individual who would not qualify to rent a car might be able to obtain one through a buy-back arrangement.

DRIVING SAFELY

In view of the numerous legal and cultural differences, safety is an important concern, and you should be aware of the following issues:

- Road signs and driving symbols will be different from those to which you are accustomed. Information describing the signs and symbols particular to a country can be obtained from the country's tourism office or the rental company.
- Get used to thinking in terms of kilometers. Many of the signs and speed limits you'll see will use kilometers rather than miles.
- It is especially difficult to get used to driving on the left side of the road. When renting in a country where driving on the opposite side is the law, practice in a safe area before trying to drive on a busy street. Don't pick up your car in a highly congested area and think you will immediately feel comfortable driving on the left with traffic all around you.
- Despite the stories you hear about the tendency to drive at high speeds in some countries, always obey the local speed limits. If caught speeding, your driver's license may be confiscated, and you could become subject to a large fine.
- Many countries have seat belt laws, and child safety seat laws are also common. Again, check with your rental company or the tourism office of the country you will be visiting for the latest information before you travel.
- Laws regarding driving under the influence of alcohol can be more severe than those found in the United States. Permissible blood alcohol levels are often very low, and some countries have zero tolerance for

drinking and driving. In those countries, having a single drink before operating your rental car could place you in jeopardy.

- In rural areas, you may experience roads that are in poor condition. They also may tend to be hilly and winding. Operating an unfamiliar vehicle (especially one with a manual transmission) on them can be difficult.
- Roundabouts, or traffic circles, are very common in some countries. Driving on them can be difficult, especially on the left side of the road.
- In many countries, you will find pedestrians, bicycles, motorbikes, and sometimes even animals in the roadway. You need to be on alert for more than just cars.
- Some cities use color symbols (i.e., red, green, blue) to designate where you may park and for how long. Failure to fully understand and obey this system could result in finding that your vehicle has been towed.
- Don't overestimate the distance you can travel in your rental car. Many roads and highways can become very congested at certain times.

You may enjoy the freedom that comes with driving your own rental car when visiting foreign lands. Just remember that renting and operating a car can be confusing and possibly even dangerous if you are not adequately informed and prepared.

chapter seventeen

Rental Car Safety

One sure way to ruin your trip is to be involved in an accident or other mishap with your rental car. These events can be unfortunate no matter when or where they occur, but they are especially stressful when they happen away from home.

Road safety is a serious subject that is not limited to the operation of rental cars. According to statistics released by the U.S. Department of Transportation, more than 6.3 million motor vehicle crashes were reported during 2001. A person was killed in a highway crash every 12 minutes, with a total of 42,116 losing their lives. Another 3 million people were injured, or one every 11 seconds.

Sadly, many of these tragedies could probably have been prevented. Note the following statistics published by the DOT for the year 2001:

- Alcohol was a factor in 41% of all traffic fatalities
- 57% of fatal crashes involved a single vehicle
- More than 50% of the fatal crashes occurred on roads with speed limits of 55 mph or higher

There are a number of reasons behind these staggering accident statistics, many of which are related to driver behavior. Although much has already been written on the topic of safe driving, it deserves some discussion here for one very important reason: whatever your chances are of being in an accident while driving your own personal auto, they're even higher when operating a rental vehicle.

INVEST IN A SAFE TRIP

When it comes to renting a car, sometimes making a small investment can go a long way toward guaranteeing a safe and enjoyable business trip. We're not talking about a financial investment here but instead a small investment of time.

Studies have shown that a disproportionate number of accidents occur within the first half-hour after a renter takes possession of the vehicle and leaves the rental facility.

There are several reasons for this. First, many travelers are unaccustomed to their physical surroundings when driving in a strange city. Regardless of how frequently that traveler may visit that city, there will exist some degree of unfamiliarity with local roads and traffic patterns. Rental vehicles are often picked up at airport locations, where the traffic flow can be particularly confusing.

When a traveler is visiting a city for the first time, the level of unfamiliarity dramatically rises, thus increasing the chance of an accident. When unfamiliarity is combined with other variables such as arriving after dark or in bad weather, the odds grow even higher.

The second reason for the high incidence of accidents early in the rental period results from unfamiliarity with the rental vehicle. Travelers tend to overlook this factor, but it can be dangerous to assume that "a car is a car is a car." Different styles and models of vehicles handle in dissimilar ways in terms of steering and braking. Even the most basic of instruments and controls can be located in places you'd not expect to find them. While driving down a strange road, you don't want to find yourself searching blindly for the windshield wiper control when a thunderstorm begins.

So how can a small investment of time reduce the odds of your trip getting off to a bad start? Here are some very simple actions you can take:

BEFORE YOU LEAVE THE RENTAL COUNTER

There is a tendency among travelers to rush through the rental transaction in order to get out of the rental facility as quickly as possible. After all, there are appointments to keep and meetings to attend. In addition, rental agents are trained to move renters through the process as quickly as possible in the interest of customer service.

By investing a few minutes to go through the following checklist before you leave the rental counter, you reduce your odds of ending up in an accident—an accident that could become very costly in terms of both time and money:

178

- Ask for a map of the area and clear directions to your destination. (Some rental companies provide computerized directions while others do so manually.) Review the directions several times to make sure you understand them.
- Write down, in your own words, some brief notes about your directions (highway exits, landmarks, etc.) that you can refer to while driving. Trying to read a map while driving is dangerous and increases your potential for accidents. Drivers who appear lost or confused also make themselves much more vulnerable to crime. You don't want to advertise that you are a visitor.
- Understand how to exit the rental facility lot. A significant number of accidents occur as renters are simply trying to leave the lot and enter a public roadway.
- If you don't carry your own cellular phone, consider renting one from the car rental company. Having a phone available could help protect you if you are in an accident or experience a mechanical problem. But never attempt to use the phone while driving. Instead, pull safely off the road and stop the vehicle before attempting to make a call.
- Ask the rental agent how to make an emergency call in the area in which you will be driving. Note the phone number of the rental company's emergency road service in case the car breaks down as well as the number for reporting accidents.

BEFORE YOU LEAVE THE RENTAL LOT

After you finish at the rental counter, you'll be directed to the location of your vehicle. Resist the urge to jump into the car and immediately rush out of the lot. Once again, remember that taking a little time can be a wise investment:

- Walk around the vehicle and inspect it for damage. If you find any, do not drive away until a rental company employee documents it on your rental contract. If you leave without any type of documentation, you could be charged for the damage it if it is discovered upon your return.
- Learn the location of critical controls so you know how to operate the headlights, windshield wipers, horn, rear defroster, and emergency flashers.
- Adjust your seat for driving comfort. Be sure to fasten your seat belt harness.
- Adjust your rearview and side mirrors to ensure proper vision.

- Check the fuel gauge to make sure the vehicle has a full tank of gasoline.
- Check to confirm that the vehicle has a spare tire and jack.
- Make sure your passengers fasten their seatbelts or shoulder restraints. Never allow more people to occupy the vehicle than there are seat belts.
- Lock your doors before driving away.
- Check for other vehicles and pedestrians before moving the vehicle.
- Test the brakes to become familiar with the vehicle's pedal tension.
- If you have any questions or experience any problems with the vehicle, find a rental company employee.

This checklist is not as cumbersome as it might initially appear. Practice using it a few times and it will become engrained as habit. You'll find that you're spending no more than a few extra minutes to significantly reduce the likelihood of an accident.

Preventing the Theft of Your Rental Car

Under the terms of your rental contract, you are responsible for all loss of or damage to the rental vehicle regardless of fault. This means that even if the rental vehicle is stolen while parked and locked, you could still be financially responsible up to the full value of the vehicle.

It is in your best interest to try to protect the rental vehicle from theft as if it were your very own. Unfortunately, this is not always an easy thing to do. Consider these statistics published by the National Insurance Crime Bureau:

- There were 1.2 million vehicle thefts reported in the United States in 2001.
- A vehicle is stolen every 26 seconds.
- The estimated total value of stolen vehicles was $8.2 billion.
- The country's vehicle theft rate increased 4.5% in 2001.
- An estimated 1 in 10 Americans has been victimized by vehicle theft.
- Your chances are 1 in 42 that your vehicle or its contents will be stolen this year.

The odds of your rental car being stolen are probably even higher. The cars most likely to be targeted by thieves are those that are the most popular with the general public. Thieves won't waste their time stealing a car that doesn't have much "street value."

Not so coincidentally, car rental companies tend to buy vehicles that also rank high in popularity. It only makes sense that the companies would make available those vehicle makes and models that the public would most want to rent. When you have a rental fleet of vehicles most likely to be stolen, your theft rate is going to be higher than average.

TIPS FOR PROTECTING YOUR VEHICLE

Despite the enormous scope of this problem, there are some positive actions that you can take to help prevent your rental vehicle from being stolen:

- Always close all windows (including the sunroof) and lock the trunk and all doors whenever you leave the vehicle. (Studies have indicated that as many as 80% of all stolen cars were left unlocked.)
- Never leave the vehicle with the motor running. It takes only a second for someone to jump into the car and drive away. (In addition, leaving a vehicle unattended with the motor running is against the law in many places.)
- Even when the motor is turned off, you should always remove the keys from the vehicle, even when you plan to be away from it for only a few minutes. (Keys are left in 13% of vehicles that are stolen.)
- Make it difficult to tow the vehicle away by parking with the front wheel turned sharply to the right or left (toward the curb if parking on a city street) and the emergency brake engaged. (10% of stolen vehicles are towed away.)
- Whenever possible, park in a secured garage, a patrolled parking lot, or near activity in a well-lit area. Never park in dark, isolated locations. (Two-thirds of thefts occur after dark.)
- Avoid parking next to large trucks, walls, or other objects where a thief could break into your vehicle without being observed.
- Activate all available antitheft devices if the vehicle is so equipped.
- Never leave packages or valuables inside the car where they can be seen. Lock them out of sight in the trunk. Valuables that are easily visible serve as an invitation to theft or vandalism.
- If you park your rental car in a parking garage that charges a fee, you'll receive a ticket or card that must be turned in when you pay the fee and leave. Never leave the ticket in the unattended vehicle because a car thief could use it to exit.
- Never leave your driver's license, credit cards, or other personal documents in an unattended vehicle.

- Don't make it easy for a thief to identify your vehicle as a rental car. Keep maps, guidebooks, and your rental contract in the glove box or out of sight while parked.

Above all, remember that although it is your responsibility to reasonably protect your rental car, never place your own physical safety in jeopardy by doing so.

IF YOUR RENTAL CAR IS STOLEN

Unfortunately, with the increasing sophistication and talents of car thieves, it is often impossible to prevent a theft no matter what steps you may take. In the event that your rental vehicle is stolen:

- Report the theft to the police or appropriate law enforcement agency immediately. The quicker you contact the police, the more likely they are to recover the vehicle. Any delay in reporting could also subject you to additional risk. If the vehicle is involved in an accident before you report the theft to the police, you could find yourself having to prove that you were not driving at the time of the accident.
- Failure to promptly report the theft to the police could also violate the terms of your rental contract and potentially void any limitation of your responsibility for vehicle loss or damage under loss damage waiver (LDW).
- Don't forget to report personal property that was in the vehicle. The personal effects coverage policies offered by rental car companies usually require that personal property theft claims be supported by a police report. Even if you didn't purchase this coverage, most homeowner's insurance policies also require that you report theft of property to the police.
- After notifying the police, report the incident to the rental car company as soon as possible. Provide the name of the law enforcement agency that took the report as well as the police report number.
- If keys to your home, office, or hotel room were in the vehicle when it was stolen, take proper precautions to protect against theft from those locations.

Remember, the car may not be yours, but you are financially responsible for it during the rental period. It is your duty to exercise as much care for it as you would for your personal auto. Even if you have insurance or purchase the company's LDW, you will be inconvenienced if your vehicle is stolen. The time required to complete theft reports and obtain a new vehicle can take a sizeable chunk of time out of your vacation or business trip. The better alternative is to try to prevent the theft of your vehicle from ever happening in the first place.

CONVERSION

The only thing worse than discovering that someone has stolen your rental car is to learn that the rental company thinks that you stole it! This can happen if you don't return your vehicle by its due date. Your failure to return your rental car when it is due back is referred to as conversion and is considered a crime in some states. In many states, there are laws that assist rental companies in recovering cars that customers fail to return.

State law varies in regard to the recovery process. In some states, if a renter fails to return the vehicle after a specific amount of time after its due date, the car is considered stolen, and the police are authorized to make an arrest. In others, the rental company must first send out a formal letter requesting its return before it can be reported as stolen.

You have a legal obligation to return your rental car on or before the day you said you would when you rented it. If your circumstances change and you need the car longer, you must contact the rental company and request an extension of your rental contract.

Before your rental company will agree to an extension, it may need to hold a larger amount on your credit card in order to guarantee payment. If the extension is authorized, be sure to obtain a confirmation number or at least the name of the rental agent who authorized the extension.

What to Do if an Accident Occurs

If you've ever been involved in an accident, you understand that it can be an extremely stressful experience. Your adrenaline is pumping and heart pounding. The other parties involved in the accident are asking for your identification and insurance information. The police arrive and also start asking questions about what happened. You become easily distracted by everything that is going around you. It becomes difficult to think clearly and exercise sound judgment.

The situation can become even more stressful if the accident happens while you're driving a rental car. Now you've got one other factor to worry about:

dealing with the rental car company. You suddenly realize that on top of everything else, you've got to let the company know about the accident and the damage to the car.

If you have an accident with your rental car, remembering the following could help to make the experience a little less painful:

- Remain calm and observant. Review what just happened in your mind so it will be easier to recall the facts later. Notice other people at the scene immediately following the accident because they may be potential witnesses.
- Remain at the accident scene. Don't leave the area without first calling the police unless you feel that the area is not safe. If you drive away, you could be arrested for a more serious offense such as leaving the scene of an accident. Always make your personal safety your primary concern.
- Immediately call or ask someone to call the police or appropriate law enforcement agency to report the accident.
- If no one is injured and the vehicles can be safely driven, move them out of the flow of traffic to prevent further accidents. Ask the police whether it is all right to do so when you call them.
- Don't get out of your vehicle unless you feel it is safe to do so. If you're in a remote or poorly lit area and your vehicle can still be driven safely, proceed to the nearest public place to call the police. Again, think of your personal safety first.
- If the police will not come to the scene, determine the location of the nearest police station so you can file a report. You should always file a police report. Your failure to do so could be in violation of the terms of the rental contract.
- Exchange only the required identification and information with the other party(s) to the accident. This includes you name, address, telephone number, and your insurance information. Let them know that you are driving a rental car and identify the rental company. Do not provide any further information.
- Obtain the names, addresses, and telephone numbers of any witnesses. They could be critical to determining who is responsible for the accident.
- Do not admit fault to anyone. Keep your comments to a minimum and stick to the facts. Any comments that you do make might be later held against you.
- After finishing with the police, report the accident to the rental company. The phone number for reporting accidents should appear on your rental

contract or in your rental packet. If not, call the rental location where you picked up the car.

- If your vehicle cannot be driven safely, call the rental company's road service number that is also listed on your rental documents.
- If you need another car, ask the rental company how you need to go about obtaining a replacement.
- Also ask the rental company exactly what you need to do to comply with its accident reporting requirements. Your failure to satisfy those requirements could result in a violation of the rental contract.

WHAT INFORMATION DO YOU NEED TO OBTAIN?

When you report the accident to the rental company, you will be asked to provide certain information. The rental company will then turn your report over to its insurance company or claim service for investigation and handling.

How much information about the accident does the rental company need? As a general rule, the more details you can provide, the better equipped the rental company's claim service will be to handle the claim. Because it is common to forget details as time passes and your memory fades, you should commit this information to writing as soon as possible. Unless you are injured and cannot do so, you should make some notes to yourself at the accident scene.

The information you obtain and document should include the following:

Accident details
1. Time and location (streets, city)
2. Weather and road conditions
3. Description of how the accident happened (including direction and speed of vehicles)

Other vehicle(s)
4. Name, address, telephone number, and driver's license number of other driver
5. Type of vehicle (year, make, model, color)
6. Name, address, and telephone of owner (if different from those of driver)
7. Name of insurance company, agent, and policy number

Injuries

8. Name, address, telephone number, and age of injured person(s)
9. General description of injuries (Complaints? Visible signs? Taken to hospital?)

Witnesses

10. Name, address, and telephone number
11. Relationship to involved parties?

Vehicle damage

12. Area of damage on your vehicle. Could it be driven?
13. Area of damage to other vehicle. Could it be driven?
Police investigation
14. Name of police department, name of responding officer, and his or her badge number
15. Any citations issued? For what violation?

Other relevant details

16. Any other details that might be important?

ACCIDENT INVESTIGATIONS

After you report the accident to the rental company, your involvement may not be over. Depending on the nature of the accident, the rental company's claim handler may contact you for additional information. Therefore, it is important that you retain all information and documentation for a period of time.

YOUR OBLIGATIONS

Your responsibilities in the event of an accident are described in the rental contact and generally include the following:

- You must promptly report all accidents or incidents involving loss of or damage to the rental vehicle. This includes everything from collisions to broken windshields. Although rental contracts may not include a time requirement for reporting, the intent is for you to do so as soon as possible. As a general rule, you should report the incident to the rental company within 24 hours.
- You must fully cooperate with the rental company (and its insurer or claim service) in the investigation of the accident. This includes

providing information, giving statements, and assisting with other reasonable requests.

- You must fully cooperate with the defense of any claim resulting from the accident. If a third party files a lawsuit as a result of your accident, you may be required to provide a deposition and/or testify at trial.
- You must immediately forward to the rental company any papers or documents you receive relative to your accident. This includes letters from other parties, attorneys, and insurance companies as well as lawsuit papers.
- Should you move or change your telephone number while any claim or lawsuit remains pending, you must provide this information to the company. Until the claim is concluded, the company may still need to contact you.

FAILURE TO COOPERATE

Failing to cooperate with the rental company or its insurer can have serious repercussions. Because your responsibilities are described in the terms of the rental contract, your lack of cooperation could be considered a violation of that contract. The result could find the company voiding all liability protection you may have otherwise been provided. Any limitation of your responsibility for vehicle damage and coverage available under other optional protection plans you purchased may also be voided.

REPORTING THE ACCIDENT TO YOUR INSURANCE COMPANY

Customers sometimes believe that once they report an accident to the rental company, their responsibilities are over. This may especially be the case when customers purchase the rental company's increased liability protection and loss damage waiver in order to avoid having to use their own insurance.

However, there is a difference between not having to use your own insurance and not having to inform your own insurance company. Even when you will not have to use your personal insurance, you should still report the accident to your own company.

The standard personal auto policy contains requirements that must be met in terms of accident reporting. These requirements clearly state that the insurance company has no obligation to provide coverage unless you are in full compliance with all accident reporting requirements. These reporting requirements are generally listed under the policy's section on duties after an accident or loss.

Failing to comply with these requirements could leave you without coverage following an accident with your rental car. For example, a customer may decide not to report the accident to his or her personal insurer because of the belief that the rental company's protection will be primary. But during the course of its investigation, the rental company discovers that the customer violated the terms of the rental contract in some manner.

As a result, the rental company declines any protection on the basis of the contract violation. The customer then turns to his or her personal insurer, which also refuses to provide coverage because of the customer's failure to promptly report the accident.

In order to avoid finding yourself in this situation, it is best to report all accidents to both the rental company and your own insurance company. If the rental company pays any resultant claims and your personal insurer doesn't have to make any payments, the accident should not adversely affect your claim record with your insurer.

There is another reason why you should always report accidents involving rental cars to your personal insurer. With rental contracts designed to shift primary liability responsibility to the customer whenever legally possible, there is a strong likelihood that your insurer will be involved to some degree.

chapter eighteen

Glossary of Car Rental Terms

The car rental industry is no different from many other businesses in having its own specialized vocabulary. But the extent of the terminology that rental customers need to understand can seem overwhelming. In order for customers to be able to work their way through the car rental maze efficiently and economically, it is useful to possess some general knowledge of certain industry "buzz words."

Additional authorized driver: Individual specifically named on the rental contract as an authorized driver of the rental vehicle. Rental companies may charge an additional fee for a person added to the contract as an additional authorized driver.

Additional liability insurance (ALI): A term used by some car rental companies for their increased liability protection product.

After-hours drop-off: Rental locations that are not open around the clock usually have some process available for customers who return the vehicle after the location is closed.

Age requirement: Minimum age at which the rental company will allow a person to rent or operate a car. Age requirements may vary by company and typically range between 21 and 25 years of age. Companies that do rent to younger drivers may charge an additional fee. There is usually no maximum age requirement in the United States.

Airport access fee: A per transaction fee that a car rental company is required to pay to the airport authority or local government if it conducts its rental business on the airport property. The fee may be charged even when the rental company doesn't have a physical location at the airport but simply travels onto airport property to pick up customers to transport them to an off-airport facility. This fee may be passed on to the customer.

Airport market: Segment of the car rental market comprised of customers who rent a vehicle after arriving at their destination by airplane.

All-inclusive rate: Also called a packaged or bundled rate, it includes the daily rate plus other fees, taxes, surcharges, and optional insurance and loss damage waiver charges. Although these rates provide the customer with a more realistic estimate of the true total rental cost, they are not commonly offered in the United States.

Authorized drivers: Persons permitted to operate the rental vehicle under the terms of the rental contract. There are two ways to qualify as an authorized driver. One way is to be defined as such by the rental contract (usually includes the renter, the renter's spouse, coworkers while on business, etc.). The second way is to be specifically named and listed on the contract as an additional authorized driver.

Base rental rate: Usually the same as the daily rate. It is the rate usually advertised by the rental company that does not include additional taxes, fees, or surcharges. The base rate will be substantially lower than your actual final cost.

Blackout dates: Specific dates or time periods (usually holiday or other peak travel times) during which certain promotions, special rates, or coupons cannot be used.

Bodily injury: Physical injury, disability, sickness, or death that results from an accident. An injured party is entitled to recover damages for medical expenses, loss of earnings, and pain and suffering.

Business rental: A car rented for the primary purpose of providing transportation for a business traveler.

Car types: The various vehicle classifications used by rental companies. The names of the classifications and types of vehicles within the classifications vary among companies.

Cash rentals: Most rental companies require a major credit card to qualify for rental, but some do have criteria under which they will agree to rent a car when the customer does not own a credit card and instead provides a cash deposit.

Check-in: The process of returning the rental car to the rental location. Rental service agents will inspect the vehicle for damage and check its mileage and fuel level before closing out the rental contract and calculating the final charge.

Check-out: The process of picking up the rental car from the rental location. The rental contract is opened by obtaining certain information from the renter (to qualify the renter). The renter is given the opportunity to purchase optional coverage and additional equipment or services at this time.

Child safety seats: Car rental companies operate in compliance with laws relating to child restraints. If the rental agent is aware that the renter is accompanied by a child for whom a federally approved safety seat is required, the renter will be required to either provide a seat or rent one from the rental company for an additional fee.

Collision damage waiver (CDW): An early version of loss damage waiver, CDW waives the renter's responsibility for damage to the vehicle that results from a collision. The renter usually remains responsible for damage that results from incidents other than collision. This distinction has become somewhat moot because many states require all waivers, regardless of what they're called, to waive the renter's full responsibility for damage that results from any cause.

Computerized navigation systems: Global positioning satellite (GPS) systems used to provide rental customers with automated directions, destination directories, and driving tips. Car rental fleets are becoming increasingly equipped with this technology. Renters enter their destination into the system and then follow the detailed driving instructions that are provided. These systems also contain directories of restaurants, hotels, and other points of interest to assist the traveler and are available for an additional charge.

Confirmation number: After making a car rental reservation, the rental company will provide you with a number confirming that reservation. You should have that number, as well as the rate quoted, available for reference when picking up the vehicle.

Contract violation: A customer's violation of a use restriction or other rental contract condition can void a damage waiver or liability protection that might otherwise be provided by the rental company.

Conversion: Failure to return the rental car when it is due back. In some states and under certain circumstances, conversion is considered a crime.

Corporate rate program: Businesses with significant car rental volume often negotiate contracts with rental companies. In exchange for their commitment to provide a minimum level of rental activity, these businesses may receive favorable rental rates, damage waivers, increased liability protection, vehicle upgrades, or other such benefits.

Credit card coverage: Some credit cards provide car renters with varying degrees of coverage for damage to the rental car. The terms of this coverage vary among credit card companies and often include significant limitations and restrictions. Credit card coverage does not include liability protection.

Credit card reserve: At the opening of the rental transaction, the rental company may place a hold on the customer's credit card account for the estimated cost of the rental to ensure that the final bill can be paid when the customer returns the car. This can limit the amount of credit the customer has available during the rental period.

CSR: Customer service representative or rental agent. Usually refers to the employee responsible for assisting you with the rental transaction at the rental counter.

Daily rate: The per day rate charged by the rental car company. It is usually based on a 24-hour clock, although some companies charge on a calendar-day basis. The daily rate is the base rate exclusive of all applicable taxes, fees, and additional charges.

DMV check: A review of a customer's driving record. DMV refers to the state Department of Motor Vehicles, from which the car rental companies obtain information about customers' driving records.

Driving record check: Process of reviewing a customer's driving record. It may include either an automated DMV check or the completion of a questionnaire. Some rental companies require that customers have driving records that meet certain criteria before they will rent a car to them.

Driving record questionnaire: Some rental companies may ask customers to fill out a form that asks questions about their driving history as an alternative to performing an automated driving record check with the state DMV.

Driver's license: All companies require a valid driver's license as a condition of rental. If a country other than the United States issued the driver's license, an international driver's permit may also be required.

Drop charge: An additional fee charged by some rental companies for dropping off the rental vehicle at a location other than that from which it was rented.

Emergency road service: Most rental car companies list a telephone number on the rental contract that you should call if your rental car breaks down or is involved in an accident or if you need other emergency services.

Express rental and return service: Process that allows customers to bypass the rental counter and shorten the time required to pick up and return their rental cars. Customers enroll in express service programs by completing an application providing basic information, which is stored in the rental company's database. Each time the customer makes a reservation, the information is downloaded and used to preprint a rental agreement in advance of the customer's arrival. Most rental companies offer some degree of express service, with some charging an annual fee.

Extended liability protection (ELP): A term used by some car rental companies for their increased liability protection product.

Flex rate: Rental agents are sometimes given some degree of authority to discount the standard daily rate at certain times and under certain circumstances. This may be done to beat a competitor's rate, satisfy a frequent customer, or manage the company's fleet mix.

Franchisee/licensee: Some rental companies operate with a network of both corporate-owned and franchised locations. The quality of service may differ at some franchised locations, where the parent rental company can exercise less control.

Fuel charges: Rental companies provide a full tank of fuel when you pick up your vehicle. If you return the vehicle with less than a full tank, you will be charged for the amount of fuel needed to fill the tank, subject to the specific fuel purchase option you selected at the time of rental.

Geographic restrictions: The rental contract specifies where the rental vehicle can and cannot be operated. Most major car rental companies in the United States prohibit vehicles from being driven into Mexico but allow border crossing into Canada. Some regional rental companies restrict the crossing of certain state lines. Failure to abide by such terms could void any otherwise available vehicle damage waivers or insurance protection or might result in additional charges.

Grace period: If a rental car is not returned by the required time, the renter may be charged an additional fee. Many companies provide a grace period (often up to one hour after the time the vehicle was due to be returned) during which there is no extra charge.

Hand controls: In response to the Americans with Disabilities Act (ADA), rental companies are required to make available hand control–equipped vehicles. An advance reservation is often required because the company may need to transport a vehicle to the requested location.

Hourly rates: Most rental companies charge a daily rental rate based on a 24-hour period. If the vehicle is not returned by the end of that 24-hour period (subject to any grace period), the customer is charged an hourly rate often based on a proration of the daily rate. The hourly rate is typically at least one-fourth of the daily rate. After the cumulative hourly charges exceed the standard full-day charge, the full-day charge will apply.

Increased liability protection: Increased liability protection is an optional insurance coverage offered by car rental companies for an additional fee. It provides renters with two benefits. First, the liability protection provided under the terms of the rental contract in many states is secondary, which means that any other liability coverage available to you under your personal or business auto policies applies first. But when you purchase increased liability protection, it will apply before your other insurance. Second, increased liability protection provides a higher limit of liability protection (usually $1 million) than is available under the terms of the rental contract (the applicable state financial responsibility limit).

In-terminal locations: A rental counter that is physically located inside the airport terminal facility. Car rental companies that are located in the terminal are often subject to additional airport fees and taxes, which may be passed on to the customer.

Late charge: If you do not return your rental car by the time listed on the rental contract, you will incur a late charge fee. The fee is typically a flat charge per hour, but after a specified number of hours (i.e., four to six), another full daily rate will be charged.

Late pickup: When making a reservation, customers are asked to provide an anticipated vehicle pickup time. If you are late for any reason (i.e., flight delay), you should advise the rental company if possible. Without such notice, a rental companies may hold your vehicle only for an hour or two before giving it to another customer.

Legal liability: A renter's legal liability for damages resulting from an accident is determined by reviewing the facts of the accident in view of applicable law. A renter who fails to exercise the degree of care required by the circumstances and defined by law is said to be negligent and therefore legally liable to some degree.

Leisure/personal rental: A car rented for the primary purpose of providing transportation for a traveler on vacation.

Liability insurance supplement (LIS): A term used by some car rental companies for their increased liability protection product.

Liability protection: In the event a renter becomes legally liable for bodily injury or property damage to others resulting from his or her negligent operation of the rental vehicle, the rental company may provide the renter with some degree of liability protection. Depending on applicable law, that protection may be either primary or secondary.

Limit of liability protection: The limit of liability protection provided by an insurance policy or other source. The limit can be stated in terms of a split limit or combined single limit. Split limits (i.e., 20/40/10) are stated in thousands and defined as bodily injury per person (the maximum that will be paid for any one bodily injury claim resulting from an accident / bodily injury per occurrence (the maximum that will be paid for the total of all bodily injury claims resulting from an accident) / property damage per occurrence (the maximum that will be paid for all property damage claims resulting from an accident). A combined single limit (i.e., $1 million CSL) refers to the maximum amount that will be paid for the total of all claims (regardless of whether they are bodily injury or property damage) resulting from a single accident.

Loss damage waiver (LDW): Not technically insurance but a waiver of the renter's contractual liability for damage to or loss of the rental car. LDW typically relieves the renter of full financial responsibility regardless of how the damage may have occurred. However, there is one important exception. If the damage resulted from the renter's breach of a rental contract term of condition (i.e., violation of a use restriction), the waiver may be voided and the renter held financially responsible.

Local market: Segment of the car rental market comprised of customers who reside in proximity to the rental location. These customers typically rent because they do not own a vehicle, temporarily need an additional vehicle, or their personal vehicles are out of service.

Loss of use: Revenue lost by the car rental company while its vehicle is out of service. If your rental car is damaged while in your possession, the company will expect you to pay for its loss of use.

Method of payment: The form of payment you intend to use to satisfy your rental charges (credit card, voucher, coupon, cash, etc.).

Mileage charge: Most rentals include either unlimited mileage or a stated number of "free" miles per day or per week. If the mileage is not unlimited, rental customers will pay a per mile charge for all miles in excess of the stated limit.

Minimum rental period: Most rental companies charge a full day's rental rate for rentals less than 24 hours in duration. To obtain some special promotional rates, it may be necessary to commit to a specified longer rental period.

No-show: A customer who makes a reservation but fails to pick up the vehicle at the specified time without canceling the reservation. Some companies charge a "no-show fee" to the customer's credit card for certain types or classes of vehicles for which there is a high demand unless the customer formally cancels the reservation.

Nonsmoking car: To accommodate nonsmoking customers, rental companies designate certain vehicles in their fleets as nonsmoking vehicles. If you are allergic to cigarette smoke (or simply find its lingering odor to be offensive), you should specifically request a nonsmoking vehicle at the time of reservation.

Off-airport locations: Rental facilities located off the actual airport property. Off-airport rental companies transport customers from the airport to their rental facilities where the rental transaction is conducted and the vehicle is picked up. Upon conclusion of the rental, the customer returns the vehicle to the location and is bussed back to the airport.

On-airport location: Rental facility that is located on the airport property but not physically within the terminal.

One-way rental: A rental in which you pick up your rental car at one location with the understanding that you will drop it off at another. Typically used for relocations, fly/drive vacations, etc. The rental company may charge an additional service fee.

Optional insurance coverage: Rental companies offer a menu of insurance coverages available for customers to purchase. The most common are additional liability insurance (ALI) or supplemental liability insurance (SLI), personal accident insurance (PAI), and personal effects coverage (PEC). A car rental company's biggest seller is loss damage waiver (LDW), but this is technically not insurance.

Optional equipment: Car rental companies also offer a number of special equipment options including cellular phones, navigation systems, child safety seats, and ski racks at an additional charge.

Personal accident insurance: Provides coverage for accidental death or medical expenses incurred by the renter during the rental period. Also provides coverage for passengers occupying the rental car but often with lower limits.

Personal effects insurance: Provides coverage against loss of or damage to some types of personal property owned by the renter or passengers while contained in the rental vehicle.

Primary liability protection: When a car rental company provides primary liability protection, that protection applies first, before any other personal or business liability protection available to the renter is called upon. The limit of liability protection provided is defined by the terms of the rental contract and is usually equal to the applicable financial responsibility limit.

Promotional rate: Special pricing offer that exists for a specified period of time and under specific conditions.

Property damage: Physical damage to or destruction of property including loss of use resulting from that damage or destruction.

Protection package: Car rental companies sometimes package several of their optional insurance or protection products into what is referred to as a protection package. A package might be offered that includes loss damage waiver, additional liability insurance, and other optional products.

Rental agreement: The contract signed by the customer as part of the car rental transaction. The rental agreement contains numerous terms and conditions outlining the responsibilities of the rental company and the customer.

Rental contract: Another term for the rental agreement.

R/A: Industry abbreviation used to refer to the rental agreement or rental contract.

Rental counter: Physical location where customers complete the rental transaction prior to picking up the rental car.

Rental period: Period between the time the customer executes the rental contract and picks up the vehicle and the time the vehicle is returned and checked in.

Rental qualifications: Before agreeing to rent a car, the rental company will verify that the customer meets its basic rental qualifications. Typically, a customer must provide a valid driver's license, meet the company's minimum age requirement, have an acceptable driving record, and present a major credit card at the time of rental.

Renting location: The location where the customer picks up the rental vehicle.

Returning location: The location where the customer returns the rental vehicle.

Secondary liability protection: When a car rental company provides secondary liability protection, that protection applies only after all other liability protection available to the renter is exhausted and then only to the extent it is needed (in combination with the renter's own coverage) to meet the applicable financial responsibility limit.

State financial responsibility limit: As dictated by state law, the minimum amount of liability protection that drivers are required to have available in the event they become legally liable for bodily injury or property damage to others resulting from an accident.

Supplementary liability protection (SLI): A term used by some car rental companies for their increased liability protection product.

Surcharge: Fees added to the base rental rate. It may be charged in response to an increased accident risk (i.e., additional driver fee, underage operator fee) or to recoup a tax charged by a local governmental authority (i.e., stadium projects).

Upgrade: Act of offering the customer a more expensive rental vehicle at no additional cost. The rental company may do so when the reserved vehicle type is not available. The customer pays the rate for the reserved vehicle but ends up with a more expensive one.

Upsell: Tactic used by rental agents to convince the customer to rent a more expensive vehicle than what was reserved. If the customer agrees, he or she pays the higher rate.

Use restrictions: Rental contracts include a list of use restrictions or prohibited actions. These may include such activities as driving while impaired, operation of the vehicle by someone other than an authorized driver, or driving the vehicle off of regularly maintained roads. Violation of these use restrictions can void any damage waiver or liability protection otherwise available to the renter.

Valet service: For an additional fee, rental companies may drive the customer to his or her airport departure terminal, thus eliminating the need to wait for a rental company bus.

Vehicle capacities: Customers often select rental vehicles on the basis of passenger space and/or truck space. Vehicle capacity is determined by the number of passengers and the number of suitcases that can fit into a specific class of vehicle.

Vehicle class: Car rental companies use basic classifications for categorizing their rental fleets. Some standardization of terms exists, with most companies using categories such as economy, compact, intermediate, full size, premium, and luxury. There is a lack of standardization among companies in regards to which vehicle models fall into which category. A model may be considered full size with one company and premium with another. Customers with a specific model preference or vehicle size need should clarify this issue at the time of reservation.

Vehicle license fees: In some states, car rental companies are allowed to recoup the cost of licensing their vehicles by passing it on to their customers in the form of a licensing fee.

Vehicle utilization: The percentage of time a vehicle is out on rent. If a car is out on rent eight out every 10 days, its utilization is 80%. Utilization rate is often an issue when determining the amount of loss of use the rental company is entitled to when the vehicle is out of service.

Vicarious liability: As it applies to car rentals, vicarious liability refers to the liability of the car rental company (as owner of the vehicle) for the acts of its renters. In most states, the operator of the rental vehicle bears legal responsibility for his or her negligence in the event of an accident. In states with vicarious liability laws, the rental company bears that responsibility even if the renter was driving under the influence or was otherwise in violation of the terms of the rental contract. Some vicarious liability states impose no monetary limit on the rental company's liability.

Voucher: A document, usually issued by a travel agent, that confirms that the customer has prepaid the rental charge. Vouchers are typically used with tour packages.

Weekend rental rates: Some companies with a high volume of business rentals may offer lower rates on weekends when their business activity falls off.

Weekly rental rates: Many car rental companies offer weekly rates that might save you money even if you need the car for less than a full week. The weekly rate may be substantially less than seven times the daily rate. If you need the car for five or six days, you might actually come out ahead by reserving the car for a week and returning it early.